THE $UGAR FACTOR¥

A GUIDE TO BECOMING A
SUGAR DADDY

JERRY BIGS

Print ISBN 13: 978-1-7335658-9-9
E-book ISBN-13: 978-1-7335658-1-3

Printed in the United States of America

Cover Design by aksaramantra

The Sugar Factory: A Guide to Becoming A Sugar Daddy is provided with the express understanding that neither the publisher, author, or their respective affiliates are engaged to render any type of financial, legal, personal, medical, or professional advice. You expressly agree that you will not utilize the contents of this work to engage any illegal activity. The contents of this work are fictional in nature. Any resemblance to individuals, living or deceased, are purely coincidental and not intentional. No warranties or guarantees are expressed or implied by the author or publisher. You expressly waive any damages whatsoever, but not limited to special, incidental, consequential, or any other damages. You agree that you are responsible for your own actions.

For more information visit: https://sugardatingbooks.com
Email: press@sugardatingbooks.com

CONTENTS

FOREWORD

When I first started the website Seeking Arrangement, I was simply solving my dating problems. I'm naturally shy and nerdy, and I've never been good with the ladies, especially pretty ones. But I recall my mom telling me as a teenager not to worry about girls. "One day when you are successful, and you are able to be generous," she said, "girls will be knocking down your door."

Over the past ten years, the website that embodied my mother's advice became the largest sugar daddy dating website in the world.

She was right. Most women love receiving gifts. For that reason, from the very beginning, Seeking Arrangement was able to attract more women than men. Today, for every sugar daddy member on the site, there are four sugar babies.

This means that you, future sugar daddy, have a distinct advantage: The wealth and success you created in life can be applied to dating and fulfilling relationships.

While gift giving is an important aspect of sugar dating, it is not the be-all and end-all. There are, after all, five different languages of love, and being just versed in one won't get you all the way there if what you want is to find genuine and robust relationships.

Also, because sugar is sweet, it attracts the best and the worst. So the sugar bowl (or community) is full of many great people -- and a handful of shitty ones. There are real billionaires and fake wannabes. There are genuine girls mixed in with desperate girls. Everyone is looking for different things, and some are willing to get what they seek even if it's through unethical means. The goal of sugar dating is to find win-win relationships, but some people just don't get it.

Being able to navigate this sometimes complex playground is an art. Having a coach or an experienced guide would save you so much time and pain. This book is it!

I have known Jerry Bigs for a while now. When I first met Jerry, I knew he really liked women, but he really, really loved expensive cars. After getting to know Jerry, I must say underneath his search for happiness, he is just a really great guy.

For this reason, when he asked me to write a foreword for his book, I said yes!

Welcome to the Sugar Bowl... I hope you enjoy your time here as much as I have.

Brandon Wade

FOUNDER, SEEKING ARRANGEMENT

INTRODUCTION

Hey bud, how the hell are ya? My name is Jerry. Jerry Bigs. No, that's not my real name, but it is the name I was given by the many sweet sugar babies I've met throughout the years. And I can help you meet girls just like them.

Honestly, I avoided writing this book for a long time. I was having too much fun. But then I saw so many of my friends mess things up with their sugar babies. They didn't know how to communicate with them and were spending *good time and money* NOT getting what they wanted. I said enough is enough, I'm going to teach the master class.

Back in the day, I used to write a sports column for a few men's magazines. But it wasn't until I made some smart investments that the cash started to flow. And I mean flow. Eventually, I quit the sports writing to enjoy the finer things in life I deserved. With it came the exquisite life of sugar dating.

Here's the thing: I'm not the best-looking dude out there, and hell, I'm pretty old, too. But when you have the right attitude and money to spend, that stuff doesn't matter! I've been living the sugar daddy lifestyle for over ten years. I've had some ups and downs with it, but I've lived to tell the tale.

But here's why I mentioned the right attitude first. Money can get you pretty much anything, right? It can get you girls, for sure, but it's not going to get you a girl that wants to stick around. All it'll get you is someone who doesn't talk to you and is just waiting for you to pay them.

Sugar dating is more than that. It's having a fun time with hot women that can make your dreams come true.

So maybe you have some money. Lots of money. But I have the know-how to get you the hottest, most interesting sugar babies in the world. And with this book, you can learn how to keep them coming back until you say it's over.

I bet you wanna learn how I do it, right?

Well, buckle in and get ready amigo! Over the next 19 chapters and probably two hours of your time, I'm gonna teach you everything you need to know.

So let's get this fuckin' party started!

MY BUDDIES....

At this point, you're probably asking, "Hey Jerry, this all sounds great. But are your friends like me? Do you know guys that can relate to my situation?"

Damn straight I can. In fact, I want to introduce you to three friends of mine: Steve, Mike and John. (These are real people, but I've abstracted their names out of privacy.)

Steve Hanson is a 50-year-old family man. He's got a good life, a lovely family, and a successful career. Oh yeah, and he's filthy rich. Steve is your typical "good guy" who loves gettin' down with the ladies. And he has a shit ton to offer. He craves adventure and wants to explore some fantasies you can't get from a stale marriage. A classic affair isn't going to work for him; he wants a discreet relationship that won't threaten the stability of his family.

Mike Samson is 63, divorced, and living alone in an insane penthouse. His marriage started off well but rapidly declined after the honeymoon stage. Single again, he's not looking to go through the emotional drama a typical relationship puts you through. He simply wants to use his massive wealth to have fun and experience new adventures. He's rich, old and has an insanely high sex drive. Fuckin great, right? LOL. Let's face it, regardless of how Mike looks -- and trust me, he looks like a donkey's ass -- he picks up a ton of smoking hot sugar babies, like nobody's business.

John Anderson is a 42-year-old investment banker. He seems to have it all: a good career, a fat paycheck, and respect from his social circles. He also appears to be the perfect gentleman. He's good looking, well-educated, confident, and aware of the latest fashion trends. However, John is still single. The traditional dating scene doesn't work well for him due to his intense work and travel schedule. In fact, over the past several years, John has made attempts to find his match using multiple dating sites. He has literally tried them all. He is frustrated with the same old vanilla dating process, low-quality matches, and the slow back- and-forth messaging from the ladies whom he can't seem to get along with. This story has been told a thousand times. The traditional dating apps -- they suck! All in all, a waste of time. Most of the chicks on there need the wine-and-dine for weeks on end and it becomes a big time suck. Guys like John don't have that kind of time.

So what do my buddies John, Steve, and Mike have in common? For one, they are all wealthy men who are in search of companionship and have trouble for various reasons finding a partner. They either don't have the time, are having trouble maintaining a regular relationship, or they're looking for experiences that are not within the normal realm of your everyday traditional dating lifestyle. These are busy guys with work to do. They love fun, but even more, they love making money. They want someone they can go out and have a sexy time with. Someone that won't nag them the next day. Someone who won't endlessly keep texting them about their next date.

BONUS TIP

To be a sugar daddy, the first step is making big money that you can spend on gorgeous women.

Here's **Jerry Bigs's Secret to Big Money Success http://mysugarguide.com/big-money**

There's nothing wrong with these guys; they just want to experience a more satisfying lifestyle. And like all of us, they wanna have some fuckin' fun, man! It's not a surprise that Mike, Steve, and John all ended up in the sugar dating world. The sheer unadulterated joy of hanging out with an endless supply of young, beautiful (and goal-driven) ladies was the perfect solution to fill their void. No strings attached, no marriage complications, no drama, and, especially, no pressure from loved ones. In a word, **EASY**.

Let's face it; guys want things to be simple, all the time. We don't want to waste time -- ever. We want to get in, get what we want, and then get out. We don't like waiting in line, we don't like fucking around and when we want a hot-ass sugar baby by our side, we want it to happen ASAP!

These three gents, John, Steve, and Mike were able to use their money to explore new boundaries and explore their sexual fantasies in a brand-new and exciting way. And there are lots of guys out there like them. The other guys may have had different individual experiences, but the overall theme is the same: a no-strings-attached arrangement with young, beautiful ladies from every walk of life in every corner of the world. Yeah, man! That's what we want. That's what you want. And that's what you're gonna get! (That is, if you keep reading the damn book!)

LET'S EXPLAIN THIS
SUGAR DATING THING

Alright, so let's slow down. Let's talk **sugar** for a quick second! You might be asking, so what exactly is sugar dating?

Well, my friend, I am glad you asked! Let me break it down for you. Sugar dating is a non-stop adventure, offering wild sexual fantasies and fun times with hot, young, beautiful women. Sugar dating is older, more mature, established, and rich men looking for young ladies to spoil in exchange for mutually beneficial arrangements. Sugar dating is where you can get a chance to explore your wildest sexual fantasies. It's college girls and single moms looking for financial assistance, gifts, and mentorship. It's all of that and more. Sound good so far?

But with all that said, I gotta be clear with you: things are not so black and white. Any experienced sugar daddy will tell you that you need to be very strategic in order to successfully master the sugar dating game. With proper execution of the great following Jerry Bigs tips to the letter, and tricks and sugar strategies, here's the pay-off: adventure, fun times, and mind-blowing sex will all become yours. You can bet on that.

For sugar dating to work, it should be based on a mutual understanding, finding the right partner (sugar baby), and developing an arrangement that works for both of you. Because it can be tricky to strike the perfect balance, this book will serve as an ultimate guide for you to successfully master sugar dating.

⚠

WARNING

The Sugar Factory might not be the book for you...

- If you're in it just for the sex, and can't handle some dating adventures
- If you're looking to game the system and cheat women out of money
- If you're going to use these sugar babies one time and drop them to the curb.

Just so we're clear, okay? Now, it's time for your first lesson in sugar dating from the expert himself, Jerry Bigs.

WHY SUGAR DATING?

OK so now we're gonna get serious. No more bullshit or pussy-footing around. Over the next few chapters, we're going to get into the important details, the brass tacks, and do some damn serious schooling. Time to buckle down, because class is now in session!

First, a little history. A few years ago, sugar dating was frowned upon. Society greatly condemned older men being involved in relationships with much younger women. It was also frowned upon for young ladies to get into relationships where they expected specific gifts and money in return. A large part of most cultures and society still holds on to the narrow traditional idea of relationships and dating in general. We're often expected to follow some very strict rules: be with someone who is close in age, and who we will hopefully end up marrying one day.

OK, whatever. That is archaic thinking.

But here is the reality of today's relationships: Things have changed - a lot. Most individuals no longer share the concept of a "happily ever after." With today's economy and the arrival of the Internet, more guys are realizing that conventional relationships where you get married, have kids, and live together until "death do us part" is a fairytale. And let's face it, who the hell wants that anyway? I don't care how awesome your wife is; it gets boring after a couple of years, right?

Nowadays, a modern relationship is all about **meeting the needs of both parties involved**. Sugar dating is rapidly becoming socially acceptable, and the Internet is making these types of relationships even more accessible. It's not uncommon to go on dating websites and to see younger girls looking for "generous older men," I know; I lived that life. And guess what? I still do!

So why sugar dating anyway? Well, there are many reasons why you may be thinking about testing the waters in the sugar dating scene. Do any of these sound like you?

- You have extra money to spend.
- You have a high libido.
- You lack time due to a demanding personal life.
- You are tired of blind dates and traditional dating sites.
- You like having a girlfriend, but do not want to get married.
- You desire to spend time with beautiful women without the pressure or commitment of dating or marriage.
- You wish to date younger women and don't exactly know how to talk to them in real life.

If any of these sound like you, my friend, then you are the perfect sugar daddy candidate!

There are lots of hot, young, college-aged sugar babies out there looking for a generous sugar daddy to spoil them. They're also ready to equally compensate you in return with their time, their attention, and even wild sexual adventures.

If your bank account total has a couple of extra commas and you have the energy to keep a young, tantalizing sugar baby satisfied both financially and sexually, then sugar dating might just happen to be your calling. It's a noble calling indeed!

In all seriousness, at the end of the day, it's all about finding an arrangement that makes you happy and meets your needs. And in many cases, what you crave from a woman is not available in a traditional relationship. That's just a fact.

So, here are some of the most common reasons why older men consider the sugar dating scene:

NUANCES OF THE TRADITIONAL DATING SCENE

Traditional dating is certainly not for everyone. We've established that. There are many handsome, successful, and extremely generous men who don't quite fit in with the typical, boring relationship standards. It could be that such men are finding it harder to conform to traditional dating expectations, due to personal time constraints and commitment issues, among other things. And more and more women are realizing they don't want a traditional relationship either. They're focused on fulfilling their own personal and career goals before settling down, so what's ideal for them is finding quick and fun dates that come with a little reward at the end.

In addition, it's fair to say that women on the relationship scene can become complacent and often have unrealistic expectations.

Your significant other may expect too much attention, demand sharing finances, plan on moving in with you, and desiring marriage and kids in the long run. This has actually become a *huge* problem over the last two decades. Women seem to demand the "perfect" husband or boyfriend who serves them at their every whim. Beware of this "power grab" phenomenon, my friend. Honestly, I'm not sure how this happened, but it's got to stop. Sugar dating is one great way to bust that whole mentality. And take some power back, as well!

If you're a busy man, not particularly romantic, and you love your personal space, traditional relationships can drive you fucking insane and leave you frustrated. This is even worse for guys who are divorced. They may not have the emotional tolerance to start the process all over again, but they love the company and sexual attention given to them by a younger sugar baby. #Truth!

Many women in traditional relationships expect to find a handsome, loyal, loving, and educated gentleman. Even worse, many women feel entitled to demanding these standards. What the fuck, right?

To be fair, the same rule applies the other way around. A lot of guys have a long list of physical, emotional, and intellectual attributes that they expect from their partners, making it harder for them to find someone who they can settle down with. I'm sure you've heard men talk about wanting a girl who:

- Looks like Kate Upton when she wakes up in the morning.
- Is as faithful as Mother Teresa.
- Is as freaky as Jenna Jameson.
- Is fit enough for you to easily carry, yet curvy enough to have the "assets" you enjoy.
- Has absolutely no "guy friends."

- Shows us enough attention to stroke our egos, yet not so much as to be nagging.
- Likes you for you and doesn't want you to change
- Makes your friends laugh and makes them feel jealous at the same time.

Women (or **unicorns** as I like to call them) don't exist like this in real life, do they? It's not like you can really expect all of that from a relationship. Sure, miracles can happen, and every once in a while you can stumble upon a **unicorn** in real life, but good luck taming her! That's a job that I never want.

Due to the complexities that litter the traditional dating scene, it's not uncommon for men to give up. They abandon the dream of finding the perfect relationship and turn to sugar dating. Why? Because the sugar dating scene is refreshingly different, adventurous, and has its own set of non-traditional rules. In light of the above expectations, you might actually find a cute classy young lady who can only be described as a **unicorn** as she is as close to perfect as humanly possible.

Unicorn: A young, single, non-crazy, sexually adventurous, drug- and disease-free bisexual female who wants desperately to live with and love a male/female couple. She should be well-educated, gainfully employed, yet willing to move all the way across the country for her "dream family." She wants to make kids and/or help raise someone else's, and, in a perfect world, possesses blonde hair, big breasts, or whatever feature is the fantasy ideal of the couple. In a large number of cases, she should be skinny, or at least "healthy," and if she could be submissive, that's a big plus. And, of course, she must love both members of the primary couple equally, and she is content to always be secondary.

How so? Well, you only get to see her on her best days, so no worries about her looking bummy because you won't necessarily be around when she does. You can enjoy her freaky side and don't have to worry about her "cheating on you," After all, you are simply not her boyfriend and you maturely accept the fact that she most likely is seeing someone else in addition to yourself.

You will have realistic expectations with a **unicorn**. That means that you don't necessarily need her to stroke your ego on a daily basis. And if you're not the most handsome guy in your circle, she won't necessarily care about your appearance - as long as you are generous. She's there for the money and support, not necessarily for your good looks. (Of course, it's a bonus if you are attractive to her.)

She knows that you will spoil her, will take care of her, and will please her in the bedroom, so she'll happily play her role as your sugar baby. At the end of the day, you will enjoy the full girlfriend experience without all the traditional bullshit and drama when you are in an arrangement with your sugar baby. How fuckin' wonderful is that?!

THE AGE GAP

It's widely known that women mature faster than men, and the age gap has been increasing over time. While younger men in their twenties are thinking about getting wasted and playing fuckboy games, younger women often look at things from a different perspective. While younger women may be into having a good time, they're much more specific about what they want and expect from men.

This drives young women to seek out older, more mature, financially stable men. In most cases, older men are more refined, successful, respectful and are much more interesting overall. This maturity level, combined with wealth and good looks, will attract younger ladies like bees to honey. In other words, like a goddamn **magnet**. If you are a successful guy with a good personality, looking clean-cut, with a fresh shave and a nice smile, then you simply need to show up and these 20-to-30-year-old sugar babies will be dying to call you daddy.

Trust me on this one.

Of course, in some parts of society, or in some areas of the country, people continue to frown on and discourage these kinds of relationships, in light of the visible age gap. Therefore, more young women are being compelled by social norms to date men closer to their age. This often results in the usual disagreements, arguments, and other childish relationship-based drama. Women are equally as sick and tired of all the games that are played by younger, less mature men play in traditional relationships where cheating often takes place.

What's even worse is that traditional relationships do not exempt women from the desire to have the finer things in life, such as traveling, gifts, and being spoiled in general. Younger men may not have the financial means to spoil them. Therefore, these women tend to become dissatisfied and seek alternatives. This dissatisfaction tends to drive younger women and single moms alike into the sugar dating scene. After all, here is where you have an opportunity to stand out, dominate, and deliver exactly what they desire. You, my friend, have the chance to swoop in, meet up and become the exact unconventional dating ideal thing that they have been looking for all along. #Daddy

With age comes wisdom. An older man's wisdom is great date bait. It means that you're more likely to understand what younger ladies want - and you're both interested and properly equipped to meet their needs. Furthermore, these young ladies are more likely to get along with you because you'll be at a higher level of maturity than the typical "fuckboys" their age. Immaturity is really a drag. Have you noticed lately that there is a shit-ton of profiles on dating sites that specifically say "no fuck boys"? I mean, women are sick of this shit. Seriously.

You may no longer have your youth, but you have something that no other young, good-looking fuck boy has! And what's that? Cash, for one thing. And experience, for another. And probably personality too.

Together, let us say fuck those fuck boys! Think about it: They are only in it for themselves. You're not. Unlike the diehard players or fuck boys of the world, you live by the golden rule. "Do unto the sugar baby as you would have done unto you!" That's your mission, my man. Amen!

EXPECTATIONS

In most traditional, same-age relationships that are headed towards a serious path, such as marriage, problems normally arise. They are due to a number of reasons or happenstances: poor communication, finances, commitment issues, and everyday relationship expectations. For example, due to unrealistic expectations and pressure from friends and family, most couples are not honest with each other throughout the course of the relationship. They either ignore or lie about issues such as cheating, finances, or individual preferences. These conflicts, compounded by maturity gaps, tend to expose themselves over longer periods of time spent together in traditional relationships.

Picture yourself as a young man in his mid-twenties. If you're trying to impress a girl your age and you don't quite have the extra money, you may be tempted to fall back on that old charade of "fake it till you make it." You may want to appear richer than you truly are, or more mature than your experiences allow. This tends to be especially common among younger men. But in the end, no matter how good we are as actors, we tend to expose our true selves and what's really behind the curtain. Most women can see right through this shit.

Let's face it man; traditional dating is becoming increasingly littered with dishonesty, drama, and stress. Ever wonder why?

Because partners usually are not open with each other from the very start. One partner in the relationship may be expecting a path to marriage, while the other is simply exploring their untraditional options and going with the flow. Furthermore, the traditional roles between men and women are rapidly evolving. Men may claim they are okay with a partner who earns more money. But they are likely to end up feeling intimidated if she's more financially stable than he is.

Women who are drop-dead gorgeous, who have a large social media following, and who are super-independent, also tend to intimidate men. Equality scares a lot of guys. And let's face it; despite our claims of liberalism and coolness, cheating is a big, big issue. Men cheat, women cheat. Why? Perhaps it's because of the dishonesty from the start.

When you look closely at the relationship you have entered into, you may realize you had been expecting something more than you got, and vice versa. So after the "honeymoon" phase of the relationship or marriage, temptation starts to creep in pretty quickly, bringing with it the nude pictures and the guys' or girls' nights out. Eventually, the traditional person stumbles upon the fun of the untraditional partner and all the trust between them is broken. And the union is over, done. It can happen pretty fast. And because of that failed relationship, money and energy on both sides are wasted.

However, in the world of sugar dating, communication is better. Expectations are pre-planned. And your arrangements are clearly defined from the very beginning. Before you dive in, you have done your advance work as a sugar daddy. You have laid out what you expect from a particular arrangement and have your sugar baby also express what she wants in exchange.

There's a pretty intense irony here: While the sugar dating scene is often shrouded in discretion and secrecy, it's actually more transparent between the involved parties than many traditional relationships. In the end, it's all about honesty and transparency. And that's a big reason why sugar dating works. It makes sense, right?

ADVENTURE

Alright, gentlemen. I'm glad you have followed me this far. It's time to go deeper into the sugar factory. So who doesn't love a little adventure in life? Assuming you are like most men, you are always down for a good fucking time. Well, if that's your passion, I'm here to tell you that sugar dating will be the absolutely perfect scene for you. No matter how you were living before, the sugar dating scene will spice up your boring-ass life.

The mysterious but wildly tempting territory of sugar dating can give men the excitement that traditional relationships fail to deliver. I mean, come on. Picture yourself traveling to exotic locations and having the time of your life with a beautiful, adventurous, young, and sexy woman - or who knows, maybe even three babies all at the same time! Now, that's what I call an adventure. With a good personality, handsome looks and money, the sugar daddy life will be yours and anything is possible! I'm living proof of this reality, because this dream life has been my real life for the past ten years. Follow my advice and you'll be a bona fide sugar daddy on the sugar dating scene and you'll have the time of your life.

What's even cooler is that you and your sugar baby will be part of an *arranged* relationship. This allows you both equally to set the rules and expectations that work best for both of you. Sugar dating allows you to simply explore your wildest dreams on your own terms. It's the way life is meant to be lived!

BONUS TIP

Want to know some of the craziest and sexiest adventures my friend and I have been a part of?

Here's **Jerry Bigs Wildest Sugar Baby Adventures**
http://mysugarguide.com/wild-adventures

You can think of sugar dating as working a job that you actually enjoy. Like any other job, there is actually some work involved. Well, you really won't think of it as work. Instead of getting a paycheck, for instance, your reward for living the sugar daddy life is getting laid. You can also think of sugar dating as a game of "choose your own adventure." It's just like those fuckin' books from when you were a kid - but in real life! Great shit.

Indeed, the truth of the matter is that most sugar babies are actually quite normal girls who are simply looking for financial support, mentorship, and a more exciting lifestyle. They want their sugar daddy to buy them things, to take them places, and to even explore their sexual desires. In addition, many sugar babies have some very clear-cut needs: they are looking to pay their way through college, pay off credit card debt, get help with bills, rent, and other expenses that you should expect to come with the territory. In some cases, you might encounter babies who simply want to travel around the world - or simply be spoiled with extravagant dinners and occasional gifts. If you are blessed with deep pockets and can line up a generous budget, and you aren't scared of a little hard work - then this is the shit you have been waiting for. You were made for this life, playboy! Read on and let's get this party started!

CHAPTER 1
CHALLENGE

Oh yeah, at the end of each chapter, we're going to get all interactive. That is, I'm going to give you a little challenge. Something to help prepare you for meeting and sweet-talking some of the hottest babes on the planet. Go ahead and fill out these questionnaires, or just take some time to answer them in your head. But do not skip this part at the end of each chapter, or you'll be short-changing yourself and sabotaging your ticket to the sugar factory. I promise, dude, these will help you in the long run.

List 5 reasons you want to be a sugar daddy:

1. ....

2. ....

3. ....

4. ....

5. ....

Pencils down! Good! Hopefully, you listed some serious ideas – and not just five sex positions! The goal of this challenge was to discover a deeper reason for meeting a sugar baby than just sex. Because if sex is all you're looking for, then you're reading this book for the wrong reasons. And that's why we are moving ahead to the next topic that you and I are going to address next.

2.

IS SUGAR DATING RIGHT FOR YOU?

Now we can explore perhaps the most important question that you should be asking yourself: Is sugar dating ***really*** for me?" You may be wondering why you should ask yourself this. Remember that the "sugar bowl" is not for everyone.

The reality: Some men fit right into the sugar dating scene. Other guys struggle to make it work and eventually find their groove and make it work out. But then there are other aspiring sugar daddies who fumble the play - and they end up getting "owned" right away by a vicious, heartless sugar baby. Well, that's *no bueno, amigo!* And mark my words, that's not gonna be your fate. Not if you keep this book by your side. No way.

As you consider immersing yourself into the sugar dating scene, here are some of the more common things you'll want to carefully consider:

THE ETHICAL DEBATE

Here we come circling back to the whole ethical thing again. While it may be borderline annoying, it's something that you will have to deal with when you dive into the sugar dating scene. Bottom line: Be prepared, both psychologically and emotionally, for sugar dating. Many people who feel as if they have the emotional high ground will be quick to say what they think. They will criticize your sugar dating lifestyle. Let them blab. Remember this: At the end of the day, the only people who matter in the relationship are you and your sugar baby or babies. Fuck everyone else. This is your life. And you can do whatever the hell you want.

What many men struggle with is the money issue: They have to decide how to enjoy spending the wealth they have worked hard for so many years to attain. Society pressures men to follow the traditional (and so-called ethical) way of enjoying their wealth, which is to share it evenly with one woman within a long-term relationship. Indeed, society exalts rich men who settle down, marry, have children, and remain faithful. They are normally considered the gold standard of traditional society.

But the truth is that your marriage can and will get boring at some point or another. If you just hate your marriage as it stands, don't worry; you're not alone. Hopefully, you have a pre-nup. To be blunt, you've been fucking your wife for decades and you may simply have arrived at the point where you want some new pussy - without compromising your marriage. Well, rest assured that many men share this same exact feeling. It's been true for me, I can tell you that. You are not alone.

Men who are more open-minded, discreet, and excited about enjoying their wealth will find the adventure of sugar dating a perfect fit for them. To be specific, the sugar scene is ideal for men who don't mind spoiling younger women by buying them lavish gifts, taking them to exotic places, and helping them out with everyday bills and expenses. As long as you're attracted to this lady, and as long as she's providing attention to your needs, then the plan to establish a mutually beneficial relationship in the sugar bowl is a solid win-win! And what kind of shrewd businessman can resist those odds?

THE JUGGLE IS REAL

In order for you to have become successful, you probably had to wear many different hats along the way. Some of you are fathers, husbands, CEOs, entrepreneurs, supervisors, or perhaps even trust fund babies. You probably already know that each role brings with it a new set of responsibilities. The same applies to you becoming a successful sugar daddy.

Your "primary life" is what I like to refer to as your daily life. This is where you get to focus on your career, your family, your children, and other essential responsibilities. This is the public life that most people associate you with. Your primary life is also the one that society celebrates, honors with awards, and puts on a pedestal. Every successful man requires a strong and solid primary life because it's typically the actual source of your income and overall wealth. Your success in the sugar bowl, however, will largely depend on how well your primary life is going. You gotta get that right first! And if you're reading my book right now, then I assume you already have that $uccess thing under control.

Your "secondary" life is your sugar dating life. How long will this last? It depends. Some men dive into the scene only for a few months, while others are in it for the long haul. The time frame will depend on your specific goals as well as the sugar babies you choose.

Balancing your primary and secondary life is very important. You see, if you lose control of one side, the other will fail to run smoothly. All work and no pleasure will leave you lonely and isolated from the sugar you crave and deserve. And we don't want that. The key here is to find an arrangement, which allows you to de-stress and momentarily distract you from the rigors of the 9 to 5 life. This arrangement allows you to strike that perfect "work-sugar balance". Be sure to give yourself a reality check from time to time to ensure you are not out of balance and losing focus on your primary life. And make sure you have a few real friends close by who can call bullshit on your ass once in a while. A "check and balance moment," if you will. That's important.

KNOW WHAT YOU'RE GETTING YOURSELF INTO

Not every man has what it takes to be a sugar daddy. That's just a fact. It requires emotional strength, financial stability, and a clear understanding of what pleasing a younger girl actually entails. You also need to be a good negotiator, because your negotiating skills will set the terms of your arrangement from the get-go. Furthermore, you should possess some innate ability to read women, know what they want, and even anticipate how they will react to particular situations. If you're considering sugar dating, you probably already know a thing or two about women. But I can't stress this enough: If you're a classic nerd that has no people skills, sugar dating is probably not for you. You gotta know how to talk to people, especially attractive women.

To some, negotiations may seem unsexy. But they're absolutely essential. I knew one older sugar daddy just starting out on the sugar dating scene. He was with his first sugar baby for well over a month—treating her to fancy dinners, nice gifts, and even paying her rent—but she never gave him anything in return. What the fuck!?

This sugar baby kept things strictly platonic, and when he wanted more, she blew up at him and told him he was moving too fast. Then, after he had decided to break things off, she had the nerve to ask if he'd keep paying her rent. That is goddamn ridiculous and *is not* sugar dating. It's pure, heartless manipulation - and you should recognize it up front so it can be exposed.

The naïve sugar daddy asked me, the great Jerry Bigs, *"Should I keep bankrolling her?"*

I had a very delicate answer for this man: I told him *"No fucking way!"* and for him it was his time to move on and find a new sugar baby immediately.

But, then he 'fessed up and reluctantly replied, *"I couldn't help it, I felt bad for her, so I paid her rent."*

Guess how this story ends? The naïve sugar daddy never got what he wanted. The shrewd (heartless) sugar baby took advantage of his kindness and his weakness and she asked for what she wanted. Well, that's just not gonna fly, my friend.

This is why negotiations on the sugar dating scene are so important! You need to know exactly what you're getting into before you start any kind of sugar arrangement. If everyone sets their expectations clearly from the beginning and explains what they're willing to give, then everything should go smoothly. If you decide to, "let things unfold naturally," then you are asking for trouble. You are going to suffer problems with miscommunication. At worst, you can end up getting exposed to your wife or girlfriend by a sugar baby who doesn't respect your boundaries or your ground rules for a discretionary relationship. Always be on your game. Don't give up the power balance. Ever!

The issue of financial stability will be covered in the next chapter (How to Get Started: Sugar Dating 101). One of the first things you should ask yourself early on is this: whether you're of the right emotional state to engage in sugar dating. Without being prepared, you can actually end up being more distressed than you were before.

Perhaps the biggest struggle for most men just getting into this scene is knowing what to expect from their sugar baby. Remember that your sugar baby is not your wife or even your girlfriend. Most men make the mistake of getting too emotionally attached to the girl's life and feeling jealous of her other current relationships. And jealousy will kill a sugar relationship faster than almost anything else. Don't fucking do that, bro.

Your sugar baby is a young and sexy girl that you're attracted to because of her looks and personality. As you would expect, many other men out there are thinking and feeling the same way when they see her. Remember that she's in this relationship for a very focused reason. But when you two are not together, she probably receives a lot of attention while you're away. If you can accept that you have no control over what she does when you're not together, then you have a healthy mindset and will easily make the transition into sugar dating.

The key: **The more you spend on her, the more control you**

will have. For example, giving her an allowance of $1,000 may give you minimal control over what she does when she's not with you. For her budget, this amount may simply take care of her car payment and monthly credit card bill. On the other hand, give her an allowance of $4,000+ and you will have more say over her schedule. In addition, she will give you more attention. It's a good idea to determine how much of her time and life you wish to occupy - and then set aside a proper budget that covers those expectations accordingly.

> The debate is real. Should you become a sugar daddy? There's a lot to consider. For example, can you follow the rules?
>
> **BONUS TIP**
>
> **Jerry Bigs 10 Golden Rules of Sugar Dating**
> **http://mysugarguide.com/golden-rules**

Feelings of attachment and jealousy are only natural, but it's important to recognize them early on and keep them in check. Assess your previous relationships and see if that is a repeat pattern - something you've struggled with. If so, having young, attractive, and adventurous girls around you may actually end up being one big pain in the ass. You may not be cut out for the lifestyle because you can't disconnect your feelings. That's ok.

Finally, ask yourself if you are strong enough to get out when it's time to leave. Are you able to call it quits in a timely, yet amicable, manner? Most sugar relationships last less than a year. Some are as short as one month. Some last no more than one day. The mistake men make is not knowing when to get out. The reality: A sugar dating relationship is lopsided. That is, your sugar baby is much younger than you and her life is just beginning. She will have new jobs to accept, new friends to meet, and lots of men to date.

In your case, you will most likely be at a very different stage of your life from your sugar baby. You should consider what is best for you when you enter an arrangement with her. Sugar babies are a dime a dozen. There are plenty of bitches in the sea (many more sugar babies looking than sugar daddies), so you always have options. Remember to feel free to get out of an arrangement and get yourself a new sugar baby whenever it's best for you. Remember in the first place that she does not expect a long-term traditional relationship, so just move along. It's easy. Cut bait and get the fuck out.

Simply follow this **sugar baby relationship checklist** to determine when it's time to leave:

- **Does this arrangement feel like a marriage**? Is it too stressful and drama-filled? Any arrangement that adds more stress than you already have with your bitchy-ass girlfriend or wife is an absolute no-no. Replace that bitch ASAP!
- **Did your sugar baby just blow you off**? That's a definite strike against her as she is not respectful of your time. We all know the excuses that they give, from their car breaking down to their pet getting sick. Depending on how well you know your sugar baby, you may be able to tell if her excuse is legitimate or not. But if you find out she's wasting your time, she needs to be dropped like a bad habit. Seriously. Get the fuck out immediately.
- **Do you often have to lie to each other just to maintain the arrangement**? If you find your sugar baby having to lie about expenses, meeting schedules, coming late, etc., it's

time to get out. The excuses and the dishonesty will only escalate over time.

- **Does her lack of discretion override your request for privacy**? Is she yapping about you and what you spend on her to her girlfriends? This is a huge sign to run, because it is only a matter of time before you get caught.
- **Does she have bad habits that involve drugs and alcohol**? This behavior is self-destructive and will cause problems for you both in the end, so call it quits before it gets worse.
- **Does she lack any sort of intimacy with you?** Does she simply treat you like an ATM? Does it feel like she is not that into you? If you are not feeling the connection with your sugar baby, chances are she is just sticking around for the money. Well, find yourself a new baby who appreciates you for more than just the money.
- **Does she get obsessed with you and has she turned into a possessive psycho bitch that gets jealous around other girls**? This is not healthy and will lead to a bad relationship. There is no reasoning with her. She is damaged goods and needs a shrink, not a sugar daddy. Cut this one off fast because this is not what sugar dating is all about.

Remember that sugar dating should be about finding a sugar baby who adjusts to your life, your fantasies, and your restrictions - not the other way around. Be true to yourself and have some fun with the process. Just know that when you recognize these dangerous telltale signs, it's time to call it quits and move on to the next baby!

CHAPTER 2
CHALLENGE

As you discovered, Sugar Dating is somewhere in between a random hook-up and a relationship. It has the advantages of both, but if you're not careful, you can find yourself trapped in something you don't want. It's important to understand, however, that everyone wants something different. While one person may want a more physical relationship with their sugar baby, others may want a closer emotional connection. To help you figure out what you want with your sugar baby, take a moment and work through this next challenge.

Answer honestly the following questions:

What DO you like about conventional relationships?

1. ....

2. ....

3. ....

What DON'T you like about conventional relationships?

1. ....

2. ....

3. ....

Now ask yourself the following: Which of these aspects are involved in Sugar Dating?

1. ....

2. ....

3. ....

Remember this: Sugar Dating is what you make it! So be sure from the very start to be clear and communicative with the girls you meet. That way, there will be no unpleasant surprises and you'll get exactly what you want.

Ready to start sugar dating? Let's see...

HOW TO GET STARTED:
SUGAR DATING 101

Attention my friend and sugar daddy in training, class is now in session!

You made it this far, so it is safe to assume that you are ready to dive head-first into the sugar dating scene. In that case, you need to know how to get started on the right foot. Sugar dating is not simply about finding a partner and starting an arrangement. The reality is that it first requires a deep understanding of yourself, followed by a solid strategy, in order to achieve your goals. This is not some swipe-left, swipe-right, mindless dating game. This is real life, no-bullshit, modern dating. While that sounds like a lot, it's actually easier than it sounds. The key is to stop second-guessing yourself and to start by approaching each area strategically. By using this book as a guide, it will get you familiar with the sugar dating culture and increase your chances for success.

As a prospective sugar daddy, it's important to get started with a clear plan of attack. Indeed, if you don't know how or where to look, you can end up aimlessly spending a lot of time and money trying to find the ideal sugar baby.

Well, it all begins with you. I know that might sound basic or even cheesy but there are several things you should have in place before you decide to venture into the world of sugar dating. So, here are three core elements you need to establish in your plan of attack.

1. CASH IS KING IN THE SUGAR DATING WORLD (A.K.A. MONEY TALKS, BULLSHIT WALKS)

A large component of the sugar bowl involves spoiling your sugar baby. The extent you choose to spoil her will largely depend on the sugar baby you actually meet, as well as your personal financial situation. The money aspect, however, is one that most men mistakenly overthink when getting started.

How much money is enough money for sugar dating? Many of the commercially published images of sugar dating only feature the ultra-rich, handsome men. We only see images of billionaires enjoying their weekend on private jets with their exotic sugar babies. While this is certainly a part of the sugar dating scene, gold standard is not the only reality.

There are sugar daddies that earn an income in the middle-class range ($100k-$200k a year). Is it possible to engage in sugar dating with a middle-class income? Absolutely! It all comes down to proper negotiating and who you choose to be your sugar baby.

But don't get it twisted; you need to be financially stable before even thinking about sugar dating. Furthermore, you also need to have enough discretionary income that you can spoil your sugar baby on an ongoing basis.

So how much is enough? It largely depends on your primary location. Uptown girls from Miami, New York, LA, Chicago, etc. may expect an allowance of $10,000+ a month. The small-town girls from Ohio, rural Kansas, smaller cities in Texas, etc. may be ok with $2,000 a month. It all comes down to the individual expectations that each sugar baby has set for herself. At the end of the day, money talks and bullshit walks. Cash is king in the sugar dating world. But you should already know that. If you're reading this, you have common sense.

As you start off, I suggest that you take your time to browse different sugar baby profiles to get a sense of what each lady is expecting. If your income fluctuates often, you should certainly consider creating a buffer for yourself so that your sugar dating lifestyle doesn't eat into your regular budget, as this will create that imbalance between your primary and secondary life, as we talked about earlier.

I have heard so many horror stories of men getting into the sugar scene without being financially prepared. And as they get deeper into the relationship, they end up compromising their own financial stability. These are the classic salt daddies (a term to be discussed later) playing in the wrong league who perhaps failed to set the proper expectations when negotiating the terms of the arrangement. Be sure this does not happen to you!

The best-case scenario is to base your sugar dating budget exclusively on *discretionary* income. This is the part of your income that you can essentially spend as you wish without affecting other areas of your budget. The discretionary portion of your income should remain reasonably steady over the course of your relationship.

There may come times when your sugar baby may need additional support due to an emergency or other unforeseen circumstances that cause her to be short on cash. If you find that she's careless with your hard-earned money, try communicating with her about being more fiscally careful. If she is not receptive, let me remind you, there are so many more hot girls waiting to find a generous sugar daddy, so just replace her ass! Remember, you're in control here, not her. At least give her the illusion that she has control. Whoever has the cash controls the game. That's the facts.

There are levels to this shit!

Just like in life, in sugar dating there are many unique levels to the game. You can split sugar daddy income and spending abilities into three broad categories: the upper, middle, and lower categories.

The **upper category** consists of sugar daddies that can easily choose to spend upwards of $10,000/month on their sugar baby. These are considered the crème of the crop - the classic sugar daddies who expect immaculate, classy, intellectual, beautiful women. The women sought after in this category are equally as picky and typically have an extravagant lifestyle, with extremely high expectations. Picture this group as the ones having dinner on private jets and cruising on 200-foot yachts for the month. These sugar daddies have a garage full of exotic sports cars, vacation homes around the world, and fine taste in art and other high-end collectibles.

Next is the **middle category** of sugar daddies, which are often referred to as "Splenda Daddies. These sugar daddies have a healthy, yet limited, budget when it comes to sugar dating. The Splenda daddy can spend anywhere between $3,000-$10,000 per month on their sugar dating, but are very selective about their ladies and are often considered to be cautious with their generosity.

A Splenda Daddy is more or less an *artificial* sugar daddy who isn't nearly as indulgent as the real deal because he doesn't have enough funds to spread the wealth. In this category, you can expect to find guys with the typical high-paying profession: lawyers, doctors, business executives, engineers. If you fall in this category, you're likely looking for a high-class sugar baby who is also equally adventurous but still has a realistic set of expectations. Don't worry about titles too much. Many sugar babies will still consider a daddy in this middle category.

Lastly, there is a **lower category** of sugar daddies. These are guys looking to spend less than $1,000 a month on their sugar babies and are commonly called "Salt Daddies." A Salt Daddy is anyone who fakes being generous to get girls on the dating site to talk to him - but has little intention of showing actual generosity. These Salt Daddies are in it strictly for themselves and looking to get the most bang for their buck. (Pun Intended.)

Men in this group are mostly average guys that earn a junior-level salary. A Salt Daddy is anyone who fakes the appearance of being generous in order to get girls on the site to talk to them. I picture these guys driving around in a late model Lexus with 100,000 miles on the odometer and their typical date location will most likely be a movie theater or bowling alley. They are normally strapped for time, as well as cash, having to request a day off to meet their sugar babies. They may also be more interested in one-night stands as opposed to longer-term arrangements.

So which one are you?

You should know which category you currently belong in so you can begin to create your dating plan and your strategy accordingly. If you are starting up in the salt category, you mind as well pack it up now and head over to POF.com or Tinder.com where your cheap ass belongs. Sorry amigo, but that's the harsh truth.

Those of you who fall into the Splenda Daddy or Sugar Daddy categories, you should start off by setting an explicit set of expectations in your profile and filter your search results in a similar manner. Regardless of the category that you'll end up in, remember that you're spending a portion of your discretionary income every month in order to engage in a sugar relationship with hot-ass sugar babies. Trust me, it's well worth it once you find your sweet spot. Take Jerry's word for it!

2. THE CHARACTERISTICS OF A TRUE GENTLEMAN

Just because you're paying for all of her expenses doesn't mean you can be a cocky asshole. Sugar babies are attracted to confident, respectful, and generous men who can take care of them. As you venture into the sugar dating scene, you should know that your character as a Sugar Daddy will largely determine your ability to attract a luscious little sugar baby. Remember that standards still exist and are expected in your role as a sugar daddy. You can't be an asshole.

In order to stand out from other guys her age, there are several important character traits that you should attempt to bring to the sugar bowl.

Keep mental notes of her behavior

Basically, in the sugar bowl, you're the one in charge. Don't ever fucking forget that. You need to be on top of your game always and pick up on certain non-verbal cues in her behavior. You should be mindful as to how your sugar babies conduct herself so that you don't fall for lies, scams, and other similar bullshit she may try to pull. As you come to know her better, try to validate her stories and keep mental notes of her actions. You can attempt to validate her stories by seeing if there's a pattern of actions contradicting her words. Not that you need to be a psychologist, but you should be able to call out her bullshit if she's asking for extra money for a "fake emergency".

This doesn't mean that you should plunge into full-on "captain save-a-hoe" mode; it just means that you should remain on top of things in terms of how your sugar baby is reacting to certain situations. The more transparent the relationship, the easier it will be for both of you. Trust me, every sugar baby has their own set of problems and you simply can't save them all. In some cases, she might be her own worst enemy. Stay away from those women! Learn to recognize behavior patterns and save yourself time and money unwisely spent on those who simply aren't worth your time and effort.

Chivalry Isn't Dead

Even in sugar dating, it's the little things that matter. Show her that you are a true gentleman. Opening car doors is a gesture that will surely get her attention. Opening a door won't get you laid, of course, but if you overthink and overdo this simple gesture, it can quickly become awkward and backfire on you. It's more than just opening doors, of course; be sure to compliment your sugar baby, offer her a seat first, and respect her as you would any other girl that you're dating. Think Richard Gere's character in the movie, *Pretty Woman*. If you respect and treat your sugar baby the right way, she's more likely to reciprocate this kindness in other ways. Be nice to her. Show her you care. Be the person she wants to spend time with. It's simple.

Honesty: Be Your Fucking Self!

Sugar dating gives you the perfect opportunity to be open and honest. Unlike traditional dating where there are so many societal expectations, you can finally stop trying to fit into a particular mainstream mold and just be yourself. Most importantly, it gives you an opportunity to be honest about what you expect in the relationship and behind closed doors. It is extremely refreshing to be able to have an open and honest conversation about your fetishes and fantasies with your sugar baby. In fact, you can even get away with this in some cases on your very first date. Be true to yourself and learn how to properly express expectations as to what you would want out of the arrangement.

BONUS TIP

There are some things that every sugar baby looks for in a man and some things that will completely turn her off.

Here's **Confessions of a Sugar Baby: 10 Things She Looks for in a Daddy**

http://mysugarguide.com/what-do-sugar-babies-want

Outside of sex, full honesty is not really that important. There is no reason to be sharing personal details with the sugar baby about your primary life. Let's face it; she has no business knowing about your wife, children, employer, home address, or net worth.

Clearly define the boundaries and stick to your guns. If she begins to overreach, remember there are more sugar babies waiting to take her place. It might be time to cut her off - for your privacy and your peace of mind.

It's not uncommon for sugar babies to ultimately become jealous. They may suddenly demand that you leave your wife and for you to start something exclusively with them, which, in most cases is not what you signed up for. Be sure to remember that these emotions can boil over during a night out, especially when alcohol or drugs are involved. When that unpleasant situation happens, it happens quickly. All of a sudden she's grabbed your iPhone and is reading your text messages with other sugar babies. Or, in full rage mode, she's threatening to ruin your marriage by calling your wife. While it is completely safe for you to keep sexual matters in your "secondary life" open and honest, you should be sure to keep your personal "primary" life *private*.

As long as you have the money to keep your sugar baby happy, you can be free to express yourself in a more open and direct manner. For example, having a weird fetish may chase away a regular girlfriend, but your sugar baby may find it naughty and adventurous. I would encourage you to take advantage of this modern style of dating where you should be ready to explore new fetishes and sexual fantasies that you've always wanted to try. Get on it!

3. KNOW WHAT YOU WANT AND HOW TO GET IT

Let's face it. In most traditional and mainstream opposite-sex relationships, men don't actually get what they truly want.

We are forced to settle and compromise. If you're too picky or too demanding, it gets worse; you'll find a hard time actually finding a partner. But in sugar dating, the rules are quite different. You actually have the unique opportunity of getting what you want. In fact, if you're not clear about what you expect out of sugar dating, then you're sabotaging yourself. And confusing her. The best that can happen is that you will find yourself frustrated and stressed. What's interesting is that most men find it hard to actually open up about what they really want. This may be a new concept in the relationship between man and woman, and certainly requires a bit of getting used to.

FACT

In sugar dating, **you need to learn how to be open and honest about what you're expecting.** You're the one in the driver's seat. It's up to you to make many important decisions surrounding the relationship, including when to call it quits. Also, remember that the ratio is actually in your favor, especially if you are in the upper-tier of sugar daddies. There are many more sugar babies out there than there are sugar daddies, so you can use this reality to be clear about what you want. In fact, you'll find most sugar babies starting off by asking you what you want. "Hey Daddy, what is your ideal arrangement?" How nice, right? Don't hold back; tell it to them straight, like it is.

There are many important decisions you will have to make during the early stages of your sugar dating journey. What age do you prefer your ideal sugar baby to be? What cultural or lifestyle expectations do you have? Do you like blue eyes and blonde hair, or does this not really impact your decision? Are you open to sugar babies from all races, or do you prefer a specific ethnicity? In most cases, you can pick and choose more specific characteristics in order to narrow down the playing field and focus your efforts around a smaller pool of potential sugar babies.

Here are just a few of the more common preferences you can specify when searching the various sugar dating websites:

- Age
- Gender
- Hair Color
- Body type
- Education level
- Number of Kids
- Ethnicity
- Language
- Location

You can also specify that you want a sugar baby who seeks a "luxury lifestyle", or is "passport ready," or who's in her early twenties. You can specify what expectations your sugar baby should have in terms of her lifestyle expectations, level of education, etc.

If you attract someone who fits the profile of your ideal sugar baby, the relationship can and will proceed quite smoothly. The good thing is that you can set many of these expectations within your profile. Set tags relevant to travel expectations (does she travel to you or you to her), possible meeting locations, and even distance limits (living within 10 miles, 50 miles etc.). Being more specific when it comes to setting up your profile tags will yield fewer, yet higher quality, matches.

It is true that a large number of men seeking the sugar lifestyle have no idea what they expect from a sugar baby. Think about it: do you go grocery shopping without a list? Well, before you dive blindly into the scene, take time to think about what has been covered here in this kick-ass book that is changing your romantic life, one frickin' page at a time. Think about your ideal sugar baby, what you'd like her to do for you, and what you're willing to give her in return.

CHAPTER 3
CHALLENGE

Dude, let me tell you, it can be hard to decide what you want when you have every single option of a hottie sitting in front of you. Some of us prefer blondes, some of us prefer brunettes. But most of us, I'm sure, prefer all of them at the same time.

Still, it is helpful to have an idea of what your ideal match would be to start.

Without thinking too long about each category, tell me what are you looking for in a girl:

Age: ....

Gender: ....

Hair Color: ....

Body type: ....

Education Level: ....

Number of Kids: ....

Ethnicity: ....

Language: ....

Location: ....

Know what turns you on – and off. When it comes to a sugar baby, don't leave matters to chance. Pick your fantasy scenario and turn it into a dream come true.

SUGAR DATING ON A BUDGET: IS IT POSSIBLE?

t's always a good idea to ensure that your finances are solid as fuck before engaging in sugar dating. The best situation is where you have enough income to spoil your sugar baby without interfering with your regular budget. However, with careful planning, you can still pull off sugar dating on a budget.

But how?

Well, it takes a combination of negotiating, patience, and having the right mindset. Remember that you still have an advantage as a sugar daddy in terms of the numbers from which to choose. If you cast your net wide enough, you can attract a plethora of beautiful, smart, fun, sugar babies who are eager fulfill your ideal expectations.

Ready to try your hand at sugar dating while on a budget? Here's what you need to know to get started...

DIAL IN YOUR SEARCH TO FIND
THE RIGHT SUGAR BABY

Every sugar baby is different. Some have strictly established allowance requirements, while others tend to be more flexible. Because you're operating on a budget, choosing the right sugar baby will be essential to your sugar dating experience - and to your wallet. Remember that you have your expectations for a fun, attractive sugar baby with a high libido. In turn, the sugar babies have their own expectations for you as a sugar daddy.

Believe it or not, not all sugar babies are motivated simply by money. I know it's hard to believe. Once you are ready to begin your search for the perfect sugar baby, you should head to the dating website of your choice and start off by using the search filters to fine-tune the results to match your personal expectations. Once your results have populated you can also choose to sort your results by "Nearest", "Recently Active," or "Newest."

While each of these filters provides you with the same results, they are organized differently. The "Nearest" option will show profiles which match your criteria closest to your location. Be careful to avoid profiles that are very old or inactive; some sugar babies may have not logged on to the site in weeks or even months. This is not always the best option.

"Recently Active" is a great filter because these sugar babies are most likely online right at that moment. Your chances of getting back an immediate reply are much more in your favor.

"Newest" displays profiles of sugar babies who most recently joined the site. In most cases, these are sugar babies with little to no experience with the site and they can be much easier to negotiate with. When you catch them early, they'll be excited by your attention and more willing to accept an arrangement that fits into your budget.

There are sugar babies who will candidly tell you what they want and what they expect over the course of the arrangement. This is fine as long as you are also very clear about your own expectations from her. Don't be afraid to negotiate. However, just be aware that if you come off too cheap, the date might be over before it even begins.

It may be tempting to try talking down a sugar baby to agree to your current budget. However, this can easily lead to broken plans. Sugar babies can be flaky. If you arrange a deal that is not very favorable to her, she might "ghost" on you at the last minute.

An attractive sugar baby may have high expectations about financial support from her sugar daddy. She may resent but then give in to the pressure to lower her minimums in a pinch, caving in to your charm and sharp negotiation skills. However, this may only be a temporary situation; afterwards, she may start asking you to increase her allowance. Be prepared to negotiate or even say no. As I have said several times already in this book: Remember that as a sugar daddy the odds are in your favor. There are far more sugar babies to choose from than sugar daddies to pamper them. You have options and should consider keeping an active waiting list of potential sugar babies if negotiations fall through.

The best thing you can do is to use the website search filters effectively. Don't fall into the temptation of pursuing girls outside of your league if you're not ready to break out the Amex Black Card. Remember your current financial situation and be sure to stick to it. As long as you use the right search filters and cast your net widely, you will ultimately find young, pretty sugar babies who will willingly work within your financial boundaries. Don't give up.

PRO TIP

If you are searching for model-level sugar babies in a major city like New York, Miami, Los Angeles, or Las Vegas, consider expanding your search to smaller cities across the USA and flying them to you. Expectations by sugar babies vary greatly by city and state. Girls in Miami might have higher expectations than a girl in Georgia or North Carolina. When you fly a girl into town, she gets an unexpected vacation – and you get pick of the littler high quality sugar baby who falls within your budget.

Keep in mind that even if you're pursuing a young sugar baby with a limited income or no job at all, you still have to come across as "the man." You don't have to be a millionaire, but make sure that what you offer feels significant and helpful to her.

Use subtle hints to make it clear you are indeed rich and have the money, but be sure to imply that you're not willing to spend it all in a reckless manner. You can ask her about her expenses and ask what she needs help with the most. If she is asking for designer handbags but doesn't have money to pay her cell phone bill, you might want to step in as a mentor to help her better understand her finances and prioritize her spending. This will ultimately help you in the long run if she is a sugar baby worthy of a long-term arrangement with you.

NAME YOUR PRICE

In the sugar dating scene, you can twist the rules to fit you and your sugar baby, as long as the two of you are happy. This means that you shouldn't be afraid to be open and honest about how much you're willing to spend. You don't necessarily have to provide actual dollar amounts, but you can say you're willing to provide an "all-inclusive" experience.

Here's an example. I know plenty of sugar daddies would never pay more than $100 to meet a sugar baby for the first time, more than $500 for sex, and more than $1,000 for a weekend-long adventure. When negotiating with a sugar baby, I would definitely not start off by offering her money just to "meet up".

In fact, I would try and avoid any actual dollar amounts prior to meeting. I would make sure I tell her that I'm generous and willing to spoil her. When it comes time to negotiate, I'll offer her experiences and tell her that it's all-inclusive and she will be well taken care of. This is a smart way of avoiding an open discussion of your budget or allowance.

Always remember Negotiation 101: **Make the other side name a price first**. After all, how can you really even put a number on the arrangement until you know if you will vibe in person? Finally, you have to know if you are negotiating something as part of a single transaction (pay-per-meet) or an ongoing relationship (long-term arrangement). That is key.

One thing to remember is that when your bank account falls short, you can make up for it through charm, charisma, and making her laugh. As long as you know how to keep your sugar baby happy, you don't have to necessarily spend large amounts of cash every time you meet.

If you find yourself in a pay-per-meet arrangement with a new sugar baby, be prepared; some sugar babies have a strict "no money, no honey" policy. Translation: she expects her money upfront for every encounter with you. Don't take it personally —

it likely means that she's been burned before by dishonest Salt Daddies or scammers, and she wants to make sure she's not "giving up the goods" without payment. She's not just an outright bitch, she might just have had a bad past experience. It's all good and it makes total sense. Try and see it from her perspective.

After you two establish an ongoing pay-per-meet relationship, she may be more comfortable with letting you pay afterward. However, you must be prepared to pay in advance if you are requesting for her to send you naughty pictures and videos, as an example.

If you're not comfortable making payments in advance and are worried about getting scammed, then you have two options:

1. Find a sugar baby who's willing to let you pay after each encounter, rather than before.

2. Talk to her about it and see if you can come to a mutual understanding that allows you both to get what you want, without worrying about getting scammed.

For instance, have the money waiting for her in an envelope when she arrives, and give it to her as she leaves. Hopefully, as the two of you build trust, you'll develop a natural rhythm to your meetups and financial exchanges that are comfortable for both of you.

BONUS TIP

Money talks, but what does it say? You may be wondering what you should be paying and what to expect.

Here's **Jerry Bigs's Menu of Services**

http://mysugarguide.com/menu-of-services

HAVE THE RIGHT OUTLOOK

At the end of the day, successful sugar dating involves being smart. If you're on a budget, it can be challenging to make your sugar baby feel spoiled. There may even be situations where she makes some requests that you're not able to fulfill, and things can get awkward really quickly.

So how do you navigate through this tricky territory? In such cases, don't be afraid to just say no. Tell her one of several diplomatic things. One is that you don't know each other well enough to fulfill such requests. Another is that suggest postponing the major generosity until her birthday or even Christmas, provided either is right around the corner. Another angle is that you can even tell her that she's not the only one that you are sponsoring. That's always a good strategy. The most important thing is to keep frequent conversations about money out of the equation. You certainly don't want a situation where your sugar baby is making you feel like her personal trust fund. Of course, you should start off by setting clear expectations regarding the arrangement. However, smart sugar daddies will avoid having to refer to their budget or their income when meeting their sugar baby. If you want to keep this hot little sugar baby spoiled and cared for, try to make sure that her dreams and hobbies fit within your budget. In this situation, you'll have perfect harmony, meaning that you will both have fun without worrying about budget limitations.

A good way to ensure this perfect harmony is to search sugar baby profiles **by keywords.** Search for keywords posted by sugar babies who are interested in what you already love doing, as opposed to those with exotic interests that may throw you off budget.

Do you like art shows, scuba diving, wine tastings, or music festivals? These are not extravagant events, but they are fun or stylish. Choose a sugar baby who already likes such amusements. This will be a cheaper approach because you're already aware of the cost involved.

It will also be up to you to arrange activities that fit within your limits and reduce any stress of going overboard. Be sure to play it cool; make sure that your sugar baby sees the perks of this arrangement, as opposed to the limitations.

What does this mean? **Put emphasis on what you buy for her, where you take her, and the fun times**. Constantly remind her about how fun your most recent experience was, and you should never mention that it was fun time on a modest budget.

CHAPTER 4
CHALLENGE

There's an invisible line between men who only aspire to be sugar daddies and those who boldly take that step forward and become one. It starts by putting your money where your mouth is. You need to know what you're willing to spend, so you don't get caught in an awkward situation.

Answer the following:

How much money per month do you plan on budgeting for sugar dating?

$ _____

How many times per month would you like to meet with your sugar baby?

_____ / per month.

Now, divide your monthly budget by your meetings.

$ _____ / meeting

This is your ideal budget per meeting on the town with your sugar baby. If it seems low, there are ways around that. For example, try to adjust the number of meetings to make them less frequent but more flashy. Remember, the better the offer, the more likely your baby is going to come back to you – instead of finding another sugar daddy with deeper pockets.

Oh, but there's one more thing. Not all sugar babies want just cash (though a lot of them do). So make sure to understand what your baby is asking for and what she needs. Chapter 5 explains all of that.

UNDERSTANDING HER WHY

N ow we get to the interesting part, which is getting into the mindset of your sugar baby. As if women are not complicated enough to understand on a daily basis, trying to navigate a sugar baby's mind can be quite puzzling. You may want to know why a sugar baby is doing what she's doing. What are her true intentions? What drives/motivates her? What are her long-term goals?

Not all men really worry about this level of detail, and it may not always be necessary. However, having a bit of insight into your sugar baby's thought process can mean the difference between creating a deeper connection vs. having a disposable relationship. Knowing what drives/motivates your potential sugar baby, as well as what she wants out of the relationship, empowers you to better align your next moves, while focusing on what makes her happy.

GETTING INTO THE SUGAR BABY MIND: WHAT IS SHE THINKING?

It's pretty obvious that men are not good mind readers. It's completely impossible for you to know everything that your sugar baby is thinking. Trust me, we probably wouldn't really care most of the time anyway! LOL. However, you can get a pretty good idea about what she wants to gain from the relationship.

Why does this matter and why should you care? Because this will also make it easier for you to plan things on your end. Sugar babies are motivated to get into the sugar dating game for many different reasons.

Goals

Women who enter into sugar dating are often driven by specific needs and/or goals which they have in mind. Contrary to popular belief, some sugar babies are actually very smart. These smart sugar babies have goals and aspirations. Most likely these same aspirations and goals are what gave them the courage to jump into the sugar scene in the first place. Sugar babies have many different types of goals. Some may need help paying for college, some may be looking for assistance to start a business, some might want to network, some might want financial support as a single mother, and others may simply want a chance to travel the world.

Any sugar baby will have her goals in mind before diving into the scene, even if it is simple as money. They may or may not share their goals with you, so you should be prepared to break down your sugar baby's inner intentions. When it comes to setting goals, sugar babies have all kinds of motivations. Some may be looking for short-term cash to catch up on bills, while others may be seeking a longer-term commitment that will result in improving their financial situation. Here's a list of some common goals sugar babies may have:

- Paying off college tuition
- Helping with rent
- Buying a boob job or plastic surgery
- Paying off credit card debt
- Keeping up with student loans
- Assistance with car payments or car service
- Spending money for partying, traveling, and other social events
- Shopping
- Networking and mentorship
- Helping to pay for her kid's needs
- Helping a family member financially

You will also find that some sugar babies have taken the time to clearly state their goals and expectations upfront in their profile. Once you're aware of her goals, determine how well they align with your life. For example, she may be looking for help with her car payment and maybe you're a financial advisor. You may be able to offer her valuable advice - just as valuable as money - on how she can manage her payments as she moves faster towards owning her car.

If your sugar baby is looking for someone to meet important needs such as college tuition, rent, or bills, you should be prepared to be reliable and committed to fulfilling her requests. You should understand that she may also have more than one sugar daddy to ensure that she has a plan B in place in case things don't work out with you. Never forget that dynamic!

Mentorship

Another common situation is when a sugar baby is looking to get started in a certain profession, and you're an established professional in that career. In these situations, your commitment to her as a mentor is valued more than just money or material things. Mentorship is also a huge part of sugar dating, and many sugar babies look up to older, established, and mature men for guidance and life coaching.

For instance, you may be a successful business owner, and one of her goals is to start a business of her own. Your mentorship could involve advising her on what steps to take, helping her create a solid business plan, advising her on how to present to potential investors, and much more. Or maybe she's in law school, and you're a high-powered attorney. You can help her understand what to expect once she gets out of the classroom and give her an opportunity to work at your law firm.

Mentorship can take shape in many different forms. Since a lot of sugar babies are in college or grad school, some mentoring sugar daddies will help them study—for her next exam, for the bar, etc. Others will use their connections to help their sugar baby get a foot in the door in her chosen field.

I knew one sugar daddy who was a day trader and actually helped his sugar baby invest her allowance and build a six-figure stock portfolio from a few thousand dollars. Other mentoring daddies prefer to simply share their life experiences, offer tips from their career, as well as provide other relevant info related to their sugar babies lives and career paths. It's all good.

It's important to know that if your sugar baby is looking for mentorship in addition to other things you give her, be sure to set the expectation on what kind of mentorship you're comfortable with providing her. For some, proofreading her latest term paper may sound like a good time, while others might not be into that. One sugar daddy might have no problem introducing her to a business colleague who can give her a job or other opportunity, while another prefers to be more discreet and doesn't want to have to field the awkward, "How did you meet her?" questions. (See Chapter 16 on **cover stories** to help prepare you for these types of questions). Whatever forms of mentorship you're willing to provide her, make sure the two of you are on the same page.

Gifts

Then there are those sugar babies who may need only minimal cash from you. These sugar babies might have an existing professional career, have their own business, or even receive some generous long-term assistance from other sugar daddies. So they mostly expect gifts and designer things every time you meet. Some great gift ideas include the following:

- Designer perfumes
- Designer shoes and handbags
- Jewelry and accessories
- Concerts and events
- Shopping sprees
- Gift cards to her favorite stores
- New car
- Spa days
- First-class flights to explore new cities
- Cameras, iPhones, and other electronics

These are just a few gift ideas most sugar babies may expect. Of course, it will be up to the sugar baby herself to tell you what she likes. You can manage expectations by using filters and keywords in your online searches. Sugar babies who have a preference for gifts over money may specify this within their profiles.

There are some sugar babies who may be expecting you to cover a particular expense, but they break it down into smaller pieces. For example, a sugar baby who is depending on you for her rent may split the entire amount into smaller portions. So if her living expenses are $2,000 and you meet with her once a week, she may expect $500 every time you meet her. You may not know this upfront as she might disguise it in terms of other requests, so make sure you notice any patterns to her expectations. This will make it easier for you to accommodate her requests without falling short of her expectations.

If you notice that she keeps asking you for money at unexpected times, you should ask her how she plans to use the funds. You may actually be able to help her manage her needs or a particular expense that she's facing. **Understanding her "why" is the first step to being able to help her down the road.** As always, clear communication and openness are the keys to a smoother, happier, more fulfilling sugar relationship.

Time Limits

It's no secret: sugar babies with goals also have timelines. If she's looking for support to pay for college, she will require the financial support throughout the duration of her college studies. If she's looking to start a business, she may need a steady allowance until her company is profitable. And if she's simply looking for gifts and fun-filled weekends, she may look to be spoiled for a few months before she switches her attention to other things.

You might have time limits of your own. Maybe you're just looking for a brief fling. Maybe you're spending a few days or weeks in a new city on business and are looking for some fun—but not looking to bring the fun back home with you.

No matter whose time limits they are, be sure you both are upfront about them and take them seriously, as they will define the beginning and end of your relationship. You don't want to be blindsided, where you're expecting a long-term engagement only for the sugar baby to call it quits after a few weeks or months. You also don't want a situation where you wish to just hang around for the weekend, only to find your sugar baby anticipated a longer-term situation.

If you have a good idea of your sugar baby's goals, things will be much easier to anticipate on your end. Don't be surprised if you run into sugar babies who have significant goals that they desire to achieve in a short timeframe. They may have to maintain more than one sugar daddy in order to meet these goals. If you find yourself in this type of a situation, make sure you know what your specific role is and how to play it.

It can be easy to get yourself tied up in an ego battle, where you end up spending way more money than you were ever planning to when you got started. Keep in mind that with any arrangement you decide to get into, that you're always in control. Don't let her mistake your kindness for weakness! This is a costly mistake.

SUGAR BABY EXPECTATIONS

Sugar babies categorize sugar daddies into six broad groups based on the type of sugar they provide:

- **Cash daddies**: Those who prefer to give actual cash to their sugar baby

- **Gift daddies**: Those who prefer to give gifts instead of cash
- **Travel/experience daddies:** Those who prefer to offer all-inclusive tours, trips, and fun and adventurous experiences in exotic destinations
- **Mentor daddies:** Those with a great deal of knowledge, life experience and wisdom
- **Hybrid daddies**: Those who are willing to offer all the above, or some combination thereof
- **Scam daddies:** Deceptive liars and fraudsters who are looking to scam sugar babies out of their time and money

Depending on the type of sugar daddy you are, you will attract a certain type of sugar baby. This is to say that each sugar baby will have their own specific expectations based on how you interact with them. As a cash daddy, you may want to feel as if you're enjoying the companionship of a sugar baby which you're helping in some way. Most men find this better than actually paying for an escort or hooker or, more bluntly, paying for sex. In addition, the thought of establishing a long-term relationship with one or more sugar babies at the same time may bring you more comfort than random one-night stands.

When you are a cash daddy, your sugar baby will have regular expectations of receiving financial support from you. It may be in the form of a monthly allowance or a specific amount that she may want every time you meet (pay-per-meet or PPM). If you wish to be a cash daddy, it's often ideal to meet with your sugar baby a few times a month, where you give her some cash during each meeting.

Without properly scheduling your meetings to fit your own budget, you can end up dishing out much more cash than you initially planned for. If she wants to keep coming back on a schedule which is more frequent than you can afford, use your negotiating skills and see where you can find some middle ground. The outcome of this negotiation with your sugar baby will help you better understand if she is really into you - or just into your wallet.

If you're a gift-giving sugar daddy, you may have more flexibility in terms of what your sugar baby is expecting. Gifts vary widely according to who gives and who receives. A good idea is to have her make a wish list of items that she's always wanted up front. Have her include her favorite brands, clothing items, and sizes. With this info in hand, you can get her items from her wish list whenever you're feeling generous so as to keep her happy. You can combine surprises with sending her cash to buy that bag or pair of shoes that she's been dreaming about.

Of course, there are men who feel more comfortable giving gifts than giving cash. Maybe this is you. Interestingly, some sugar babies perceive this as you being more of the "traditional" type. They may take you as being more grounded in the boyfriend/girlfriend-like relationships based on the gifts you offer. This can be both a good thing and a bad thing.

It can be a good thing if your sugar baby is content with receiving gifts on a regular basis. For example, sugar babies who are mostly looking for fun times may feel content with gifts of all kinds, making it unnecessary for you to give them actual cash. However, most sugar babies will expect actual cash in addition to, or in place of, gifts. It may be in your best interests to be a "hybrid" daddy, where you provide both cash and gifts in accordance with your actual budget. This will create a perfect balance for the needs of your sugar baby.

Regardless of their goals, they can use the actual cash to buy what they want/need (while keeping your gifts for sentimental value). Most sugar babies will be more attracted to hybrid daddies right off the bat. While it may seem difficult at first, try to find the right balance between both cash and gifts. Remember that you can negotiate all parts of this arrangement, so don't hold back on asking her what she expects and telling her specifically what you're willing to offer.

BONUS TIP

We know a lot from experience. But sometimes it's good to just ask.

Here's **Confessions of a Sugar Baby: Why She Does It**

http://mysugarguide.com/why-she-does-it

WHAT AGE RANGE OF MEN ARE THEY LOOKING FOR?

Do sugar babies consider the age of sugar daddies? Do they take age seriously? This is a debate that continues to rage on in the sugar dating world.

By definition, a sugar daddy can really be of any age. What's important is *the role that he's playing in the relationship,* which is providing for his sugar baby. In fact, there are some rare arrangements where the sugar baby is actually older than her sugar daddy. However, the norm is that sugar babies look for sugar daddies because they're mature, smart, and rich. These qualities are much harder for them to find in men their own age.

What most men wonder is whether you have to be of a certain age to attract certain sugar babies. The truth is that there is not a golden age for sugar dating. Every sugar baby will have her own preferred age range, and each sugar daddy will enter the sugar dating scene at various stages of life. As a rough guideline, here are some common age ranges and life situations where men end up in the sugar dating scene:

Men under 30

In most cases, if you're considering sugar dating and you're under 30 years old, it's seen by others as experimenting. You may simply want to test the waters and see what these young beautiful girls have to offer. Every sugar dating website requires that all users, both men and women, are at least a minimum of 18 years old. The "under 30" crew may have achieved success early in their lives (making over $100k at this age) or they may have trust funds which they can dip into for cash to fuel their sugar dating desires. While most sugar dating websites do not provide income verification, some in this age range tend to simply lie about their income. These "fake it till you make it" sugar daddies typically do not last long before they need to head back to Tinder.

As a young sugar daddy, your experiences will be bittersweet. Bitter in the sense that sugar babies may be confused as to why you're looking to enter the scene at such a young age. Some might even see it as a red flag. It's also bitter in the sense that they may not think you have as much to offer as other "more traditional" and older sugar daddies.

We discussed the maturity gap earlier that leads younger women to seek out older men, rather than guys who are closer to their own age. Because of this, you may find it trickier to land a sugar baby due to the age gap that some sugar babies desire. But of course, there are plenty of sugar babies who don't care. It all comes down to your occupation, income, generosity, level of maturity, and looks. Most sugar babies are looking for men closer to 40 and up. But if you fit their preferred qualities, you will certainly attract plenty of sugar babies.

Depending on your ability to express your intentions and to be open and honest, you can actually enjoy the perks of being young and in "the sugar game." Being closer in age to your sugar baby means that you may enjoy the same experiences, exchange interesting conversations during dinner, and even have a more exciting sex life.

Furthermore, your sugar baby may be genuinely attracted to you during the relationship, as opposed to having to "endure" your presence in a more discreet vs. public fashion. If she falls for you, then bam! You've hit the jackpot, provided you're looking to settle down. If you decide to settle down, chances are you will spend far less money and possibly even develop something closer to a traditional relationship.

Men 31- 39

Men of this age range are most commonly married with children. Some may be recently divorced, while others are just looking for a fling to spice things up. If you're in this age range, you will be right in the sweet spot for most sugar babies. Most young girls view men in this age range as financially stable and capable of spoiling them as they desire. These men are also more likely to maintain longer sugar baby relationships based on their personal and professional lives.

You can take advantage of being in this age bracket to land young and pretty girls of your dreams. Just be open and honest about what you expect, and make sure you communicate these same intentions to your sugar baby.

Men 40 or older

If you're in this age bracket, you may have never been married, are divorced, or you're not interested in a traditional relationship. You may have been divorced and are not planning to remarry based on the emotional and financial commitment involved. In this age range, you will find it easier to land a sugar baby. You may have even had a sugar baby before and you've become familiar with some of the challenges that comes with the territory of sugar dating.

At this age, you're in your prime for sugar dating. If you're in this age bracket and you also earn good money, the sugar babies will come pouring in. You'll just have to filter through their profiles to select the right one. Have an income of over $1 million in this age bracket? Then consider yourself "the king" of the sugar dating world.

Many sugar babies view men in this age range as financially secure, experienced, mature, and ready to spoil them. Either way, know that you're a stud in the sugar dating scene and take full advantage of it in order to find the best sugar baby out there for you.

CHAPTER 5
CHALLENGE

So, what kind of Daddy are you? Answer these questions to give yourself a clearer idea:

Would you prefer giving your baby cash or a gift?

Do you have anything you can offer your baby outside of cash or gifts (i.e. mentorship/training/financial help etc.)

Are you okay with a sugar baby with a time limit or are you looking for a longer commitment?

What age range do you fall into?

We can't tell you exactly what kind of Daddy you will become. It's really up to you. But by answering these questions, you're a step ahead of most. And let me tell you, I've known a good amount of friends who get into a sugar situation without knowing what they want, and all of a sudden they're overwhelmed by sugar baby proposals.

Pat yourself on the back, dude; you're almost there. Now, let's land that first sugar baby!

HOW TO LAND YOUR
FIRST SUGAR BABY

We have already covered a lot of information in the first five chapters about what to expect from the sugar dating scene. It's now time for a more practical approach. Are you ready to start the process of finding your first sugar baby? This section will guide you through the best sugar dating platforms available.

If this is the very first time for you, it can bring up a mix of many different emotions. You may be excited and eager to meet your "arm candy." At the same time, you may also be nervous about what to expect, what her expectations will be, and how the relationship will unfold moving forward.

Fellas, don't worry! You're working with Mr. Bigs and we will take it one step at a time in this book. Here are some of the most common ways through which you can meet a sugar baby.

1. ONLINE: VIA WEBSITES AND MOBILE APPS

Thank God for the Internet. Nowadays, sugar dating has become much easier to discover and match with new talent through the use of niche dating websites that connect sugar babies with sugar daddies. How do they work? Very simple: you register an account, fill out your profile, upload a photo, enter the relevant information, and the website matches you with the most suitable sugar babies from your own backyard to across the globe. Think of it as a dating site specifically for sugar relationships.

Here are some of the most popular sugar dating websites used.

Seeking *(http://mysugarguide.com/seeking)*
Arguably the most popular sugar dating site in the world, Seeking boasts one of the Internet's most smoking collections of sugar babies online. That's because it's easy for these gorgeous, financially-challenged baddies to sign up. It's free for college students and $20 a month for non-students. Daddies and mommas pay $90 a month. That's not bad at all, considering this is the Cadillac of sugar dating.

Ashley Madison *(http://mysugarguide.com/ashleymadison)*
Since the dating and affair pioneer's data breach in 2015, they've recovered and more than doubled their membership to 52 million worldwide. They've also expanded their focus from helping organize discreet affairs to sugar relationships as well, making them a trusted name in the sugar community.

Secret Benefits *(http://mysugarguide.com/secretbenefits)*
Secret Benefits is both new *and* full of legit sugar babies,

making it a frikkin' unicorn right off the bat. They also guarantee your confidentiality, which is a load off when you want to keep your sugar life discreet.

Miss Travel *(http://mysugarguide.com/misstravel)*

Here's the perfect place for generous travelers looking for attractive companions to join them on their adventures. Miss Travel makes it simple for international hotties to find giving companions to fund their travels. Free for all to join, but daddies and mommas have to upgrade to send messages.

What's Your Price *(http://mysugarguide.com/whatsyourprice)*

Feature-packed, free to join, and a transformative approach to dating have earned What's Your Price special attention from both the sugar dating scene and leading journals like *Forbes.* It's a straightforward process: 1) Find a hottie you fancy and 2) Make a bid up to $500 to 'win' a date with her. You can also buy tokens to chat with your potential dates in advance so you know what you're getting into.

Sugar Daddie *(http://mysugarguide.com/sugardaddie)*

An oldie but a goodie. Sugar Daddie has a great reputation among generous daddies for its female-only sugar baby rule. Add in the fact that all profiles are manually reviewed by the staff and what do you get? Quality hotties galore ripe for the taking, my friend.

Victoria Milan *(http://mysugarguide.com/victoriamilan)*

The perfect response to Ashley Madison's 2015 data leak: Victoria Milan's strict "no identifying info" rule has made it intensely popular in the sugar scene for people looking to keep things quiet. It's a European site, but don't let that keep you from checking out the fine array of babes they have available.

Sugar Daddy *(http://mysugarguide.com/sugardaddy)*

You'd think this site would be an old player, but it only just hit the scene in 2017. Despite its crappy site design, it's jumped up through the ranks quickly and earned a spot as one of the top sugar dating sites out there.

Rich Meet Beautiful *(http://mysugarguide.com/richmeetbeautiful)*

The name makes it perfectly clear what the site is about so you don't need to sift through the riff-raff to find the gem. And because nearly every profile is manually reviewed, you know you're only spending your time on quality girls who know what they're doing.

Sugar Daddy Meet *(https://www.sugardaddymeet.com/)*

As of January 2019, newcomer SugarDaddyMeet boasts over 1,656,770 sugar babies and only 406,860 sugar daddies. That's an amazing ratio! The site only accepts wealthy daddies and attractive women which helps cut through the BS.

Established Men *(https://establishedmen.com/)*

One of the best places for college girls to find older, more interesting, and respected men in search of younger, attractive companions. The hotties here get both registration and premium features for free while businessmen and entrepreneurs pay to browse the smoldering selection of sugar babies.

> **BONUS TIP**
>
> Most websites make you sign up before getting a feel for the site. We thought we'd provide you with an inside look.
>
> *Here's* **A Preview into The Best Sugar Dating Sites**
>
> **http://mysugarguide.com/website-preview**

The best thing about sugar dating websites is that the ratio is always in your favor as the sugar daddy. Yes, you read that right; there are many more sugar babies out there looking for you than there are men looking for sugar babies. This means that if you play your cards right, you can maximize your chances of landing a sugar baby who meets your expectations.

However, a bigger selection pool can also lead to its own set of problems. If you jump into the sugar bowl without a solid game plan, you can end up selecting the wrong partner, or even worse, ruining your personal reputation. Remember that you only have one shot at making a lasting first impression. If you pretend to be a sugar daddy and don't honor your end of the arrangement, this type of behavior will quickly ruin the image your profile portrays. Over time this type of behavior will significantly reduce your chances of landing a high-quality sugar baby as you will be labeled as a salt daddy or scammer. Keep in mind that some of the girls, also known as "sugar sisters," know each other well, and word travels fast. They may be attending the same college, work together, or run in the same social circle. Sugar sisters talk, and one negative experience with a scamming sugar daddy can ruin your future chances with many more sugar babies.

So how can you begin to navigate the online world of sugar

dating? It first begins with understanding the sugar baby profiles in order to adjust your own strategy and profile accordingly. Let's first begin with the upper echelon; Sugar babies who expect lavish gifts, stacks of cash, and first-class spoiling.

How can you spot their profiles? They will be open and honest about what they expect to receive. Most of them are experienced in this space and they know how to negotiate effectively to get what they want. Their profiles will include hobbies such as travelling, shopping, working out, etc. They may also have appeared in television ads, magazines, adult films, or have a large social media following. With their open and upfront expectations, you have the option to evaluate their profiles and decide if this is the way to go. Be sure to read over their entire profile before sending a potential sugar baby your well-thought-out introductory message.

Perhaps the most promising group for both newer and experienced sugar daddies is the college-aged group of sugar babies (or those who are fresh out of college). The good thing about these girls is that they're typically open to sexual exploration, and they're in the sugar dating scene for money, new experiences, and fun-filled events.

This means that you're in a good position to get what you want as you satisfy their financial needs. This group of girls is also less likely to be overly demanding in terms of what they expect from you. They may have less experience in the sugar bowl, or they don't quite understand their true "sugar value." What typically happens is that, over time, these newbies start getting lots of attention on various sugar websites and they slowly but steadily begin to raise their expectations over time. If you act quickly enough, you can grab yourself a very fine, young beauty who won't "drain the bank" during her early days in the sugar baby game.

How can you spot these profiles? Look closely at the "Occupation Industry" segment of each profile. If you see job titles such as server, nanny, office assistant, student, etc., you're right where you belong. You may also notice that in their descriptions, they may share information about themselves and what they bring to the table. It's not just about her, it's also about what you're getting. This, for you, is very important. You want a sugar baby who also cares about your needs and understands that this is a mutually beneficial arrangement.

Be wary of those girls who simply talk about what they want and leave it at that. How can you spot this quickly? The best thing to do is message them and gauge their responses. Some may not disclose much because of privacy reasons, especially if they're still in school. Filter these profiles by age, education and location so you can begin messaging the best candidates available. Use the keywords "student, school, college, tuition, university, degree and/or studying."

When it comes to sugar dating sites, filters are your best friend. Filters allow you to search for exactly what you're looking for, so you don't waste your time browsing through a bunch of profiles that aren't right for you. If you're looking for a pay-per-meet type of arrangement, rather than providing a regular allowance, you can set your filters to find girls interested in the same type of arrangement. You can also use filters to find certain characteristics, or exclude certain others. The specific filters available to you when searching will ultimately come down to which site you join.

For instance, say you're not into a particular body type. ("Curvy" sounds like you might have nice curves in the right places, but to a lot of people, it's just a politically correct word for "fat.") You can set your filters so it doesn't show you those body types you do not favor. It may seem shallow, but what's the use of wasting your time with someone you just don't find attractive? The more filters you use, the less results come up, but you will be presented with sugar babies who fit exactly the criteria you're looking for.

In some cases, you will come across profiles of sugar babies simply looking for companionship or someone to cure their boredom. Contrary to the myths about most sugar babies, they are here to have someone spoil them, take them out to new and fancy places, and occasional trips out of town. They may not even expect money during each meet-up, as they're also interested in having fun (which could include wild sexual adventures). This is often a pretty good deal for any sugar daddy, but remember to set appropriate boundaries.

Most of the sugar babies in this category tend to be either new in town, have experienced a recent breakup, are broke, desperate, or even a bit crazy, meaning that they can easily become attached and expect more from you emotionally than you are willing to give. Proceed with caution!

MEETING SUGAR BABIES THROUGH FRIENDS

Many people have met their current girlfriend or wife through a friend. Well, the same logic can apply to sugar dating. It's not uncommon for you to meet a sugar baby through a friend who you know in the scene, or even one of your current sugar baby's friends. Networking is a significant part of sugar dating, and it's not uncommon for people to meet new sugar babies through people they already know in the scene. In fact, many girls are introduced into sugar dating by a friend who has already been in the sugar bowl for some time.

As a sugar daddy looking for your first sugar baby, it may help to know a buddy who is a successful sugar daddy. He might be able to connect you with a friend of one of his past or present sugar babies. This is a great way for you to get your feet wet in the sugar dating scene without having to spend all of your time hunting and searching on the various sugar dating websites. Consider yourself lucky to have a friend who is already experienced in what you're about to get yourself into, because they can provide valuable advice and helpful tips in the sugar dating world.

The good thing about friendly hookups is that you're more likely to be comfortable from the get-go. There's no pressure in meeting your sugar baby and sharing what you expect from them and what you can give them in this arrangement. Even though you get to bypass the traditional search process, you should not forget to discuss your arrangement expectations with your new sugar baby. Of course, the success of this strategy will largely depend on the people who are facilitating the hookup and their pool of available sugar babies. Be sure that they take into consideration your preference for looks, personality, and style.

To some degree, you're entrusting your buddy to ensure that his current sugar baby finds a good match for you. It may require a little bit of luck to find a hot sugar baby, but it's almost always a safe bet. At the end of the day, you're depending on your friend's taste, so don't be afraid to jump in headfirst and do your own research in order to ensure you get exactly what you want.

CHAPTER 6
CHALLENGE

Time to nut up or shut up, boys. I want you to go out there and visit each and every one of the websites above. I don't care if one doesn't sound like your cup of tea. You need to figure out what suits you best.

When you're ready, sign up for the premium membership for at least three of the top sites. If you really want results, sign up for all of them. I know, I know - but you'll need a membership to even use the site anyway. That's just how this game works. Besides, a sugar daddy like yourself wouldn't let something small, like a monthly membership, stand between them and a goldmine of beautiful sugar babies. That's salt daddy shit.

Now, I can predict plenty of success with all of these sites. But my hands-down favorites are Seeking, Secret Benefits, and Miss Travel. Each has more than enough different types of smoking hot women to be worth your time. They give you more features for your money, which makes it easier to nail down the perfect honey to carry around on your arm.

Make no mistake; your results will vary from others, depending on your location and what you're looking for. That's why I want you to check out what each one has to offer. If you didn't give each site a fair chance, and this doesn't work, don't come crying to me. Jerry Bigs gives great advice. But you have to follow it to succeed.

Trust me, readers; if an ugly, old bastard like me can make this work, there's no reason you can't! #truth

I'll make this even easier for you. Sign up through the links provided and you'll get priority access when you join.

Need another reason? Head over to SugarDatingReviews.com for in-depth reviews of each site listed above by yours truly.

I can't make this any simpler for you. Now put this book down (but hey, just momentarily), then go out there and start your website search. Take a look at the beautiful women waiting to hear from a generous sugar daddy like yourself.

7.

CREATING YOUR ONLINE SUGAR DATING PROFILE: A STEP-BY-STEP GUIDE

Here's a deeper perspective on creating your very first online profile. Getting started on a website can be quite confusing, intimidating, and sometimes time-consuming. Rather than spending hours clicking around, here's a step-by-step guide that will help you create a stellar profile in a shorter amount of time.

WHAT DOES A TYPICAL PROFILE INCLUDE?

For most websites, a profile is composed of a user name, your headline, an "about me" section, and a "what you're looking for" section. Let's look at each section, one by one.

Creating a username

Usernames are perhaps the trickiest part of any sugar dating online profile. You need a sugar dating profile that doesn't expose your real name for all to see, but is also not a cliché like "Dream Lover." So how do you avoid using a cliché username that will get you zero attention? Here's where your imagination needs to kicks in.

Your username should reflect your ability to stand out from the pack. For example, any system-generated username such as "Superman3456" will not stand out to most sugar babies. Avoid these types of usernames and focus on names that have not been taken by anyone. Also, don't get into the trap of usernames that are too obvious, such as "Sugar_Daddy1" or "Username Taken1."

So what username should you use? Look for something that's a perfect balance between wit, fun, and intent. Here are some good examples you can twist in your own way:

- Rich Homie Steve
- Lady Spoiler
- BetterThanYourLastGuy
- The Sugar Dr
- Amex Black Card
- LetsGoAdventure
- Your Last SD
- Professional Lover
- UnicornHunter11
- FerrariDriverDave

You can also use a fake name or your middle name.

The Headline

Your headline is exactly what it is; it's an actual headline, imagine that. Think of it as a one-liner that should entice that perfect sugar baby to open and read your profile. When creating a headline, emojis are useful for grabbing attention. When possible, use an emoji that represents you and your interests. Also, think of your headline as the news. In the old days, a poorly written headline with no humor or mystery wouldn't get you to read the article. Now translate that into current times, where sugar babies have attention spans shorter than that of a goldfish. If your profile headline isn't clever and intriguing, then the bottom line is that the chicks won't click and they won't learn what you're all about. When you don't catch their attention almost immediately, then you miss out on your potential match.

The trickiest part in creating a headline is that you need to make it short, sweet, and clever. If it's too wordy, it may not make sense at first glance and women will move on to the next profile. If it's too boring, it won't grab her attention. And if it's too inappropriate, it might just turn her off.

So what's the perfect headline? A good strategy that often works is to use brief sentences that are attention-grabbing and easy to read.

Check out these sample headlines:
- Let's throw a dart at the map!
- I'm living your dream, so come join me!
- Gym lover looking for a fit sugar baby
- Adventure daddy; have your passport ready!
- A, B, C, E - looking for the D?
- Money can't buy happiness, it buys Birkin
- Experienced daddy wants to spoil you
- Whatever you want
- Generous guy. No drama!
- Jet-setter looking for perfect travel partner
- Seeking sugar, not cavities
- Willing to lie about where we met
- Free 30-day trial

- Blue eyes, blonde hair, and a big budget
- Like long walks to the bank?
- I have 2 nightstands... next to my bed
- Your boyfriend is broke! I'm not.

The "About me" section

Now, this is the part of your profile where you must "put it all on the table." There's no turning back now! Basically, as soon as a sugar baby decides to click your profile, she will go right to your About Me section. This is where you have to close the deal, make the sale, etc. Here's where must give her a good idea about who you are, what you have to offer, and why you're better than all those other guys on this website.

However, you should not consider this the place where you're robotically listing your accomplishments, as you would in a resume. In fact, the About Me section should be fun, free-spirited, and engaging, tailormade to the type of sugar baby you're looking to attract. Keep in mind that nobody wants to read five hundred words about your career and life. Keep it short and sweet, and make sure to include relevant keywords that will attract potential sugar babies with similar interests listed in her own description.

Don't make it bland and boring. Make it light and fun, but not ridiculous. Share interesting facts about yourself and what you love to do. Explain how your personality and attributes will guarantee that your sugar baby will enjoy herself more than she has with any previous sugar daddies. While you are tooting your own horn loudly, be sure to moderate the volume! Avoid being overly braggadocious. Tie in what you have to offer with what is fun and unique about yourself.

For example, if you're telling a potential sugar baby that you're willing to travel with her around the country, mention some of your favorite destinations and how the return trip will be ten times better with a beautiful, traveling sugar baby. Tie in any interesting experiences you may have had in the past in this country, and hint at how the next trip will also benefit this globe-trotting sugar baby.

Here are some examples of **activities** to add in this section.

- Shopping
- Music festivals
- Concerts
- Fitness
- Fine dining
- Boating
- Sporting events
- International travel

Don't shy away from adding a brief list of traits that you're looking for in sugar babies. What do you like in terms of height, ethnicity, weight, body size, hobbies, etc.? Also, be sure to include your "deal breakers" - because knowing what you don't want is as important as knowing what you do want! Hell, why waste your valuable time reading through countless profiles that you're not interested in? Some common deal breakers are tattoos, piercings, small boobs, height, age, and ethnicity.

Here's an example of a really effective and readable "About Me" section.

I am a force to be reckoned with because I am full of positive energy. I'm an intellectual, creative, artistic, musical, not to mention very successful and romantic. I am looking for an open-minded, fun, loving woman who is a young professional yet wants to escape her everyday life. When I find the right one, I'm willing to show her a whole new world of excitement and adventure. I can spoil her with shopping, boating, and 5-star dinners. I'm not looking to settle down just yet, but I am willing to be a reliable sugar daddy that you can count on. I love to travel and exotic island destinations are among my favorite. I enjoy music festivals and go to Ultra Miami and EDC Vegas annually. My ideal woman should be:

- *At least 5'4" or taller*
- *I prefer Blondes over Brunettes but not a deal breaker*
- *My ideal sugar baby will be between 22-29 years old*
- *Living within 50 miles of Miami*
- *No large visible tattoos*
- *I am a boobs guy, but don't worry if you don't have big boobs, I am happy to help you fix that*
- *Sexually adventurous*

Keep it upbeat! Too many people make the common mistake by complaining in their profiles. This is a major turn-off to sugar babies. Imagine looking at a sugar baby's profile and it's full of bitching about how her past sugar relationships didn't meet her needs, blah blah blah. You would probably dismiss her as being a full-on negative and toxic bitch. So imagine when it's the other way around, and you're putting out bummer vibes that will make sugar babies think of you as the male version of Debbie Downer. It's certainly not a good look for your profile.

So what's the winning message? Keep it fun, light-hearted, personal, and interesting. Of course you can throw in a couple of humblebrags - so long as you do so in a clever way.

The "What you're looking for" section

Here's another section where you have the chance to tailor your message to attract sugar babies that fit your ideal expectations. But, if poorly written, it can become the section where you can end up chasing them all away. So what are you looking for? You're probably looking for many different qualities: sexy, self-confident, fit, kind-hearted, goal-driven, and much more. However, most sugar daddies make the mistake of not clearly stating what qualities they are looking for in their sugar baby.

Women are detail-oriented. They pay attention to feedback. So, it should come as no surprise that most ladies pay close attention to what you expect from them, and they can be very hard on themselves as they self-assess their own qualities. Going into too much detail in this section puts you at risk of chasing away a sugar baby who may actually be a great fit for you. So how do you find a happy medium? Here are a few tips:

Keep things simple: Keep it simple, stupid. State general qualities that you're looking for in a sugar baby, but don't overemphasize every little detail. For example, you may list that you're looking for a fun, outgoing, and physically fit sugar baby. But don't go into too many specifics. Remember that you want to maintain a certain level of generalization so that sugar babies still feel comfortable to message you. Give them a rough idea, but don't make your qualifications impossible.

Tags

When first creating your profile on Seeking, you'll be asked to select seven of approximately thirty tags. These include Emotional Connection, Passport Ready, Romance, No Strings Attached, Luxury Lifestyle, and many more.

While you want to choose tags that are relevant to you, don't feel as this is the be-all and end-all of your profile. If anything, this section will help show you profiles in your search with similar tags. You may also search tags to find women who more closely share your interests.

Public and Private photos

Now comes the photos section. Yes, one of the most important parts of your profile. Have you ever heard the phrase "don't judge a book by its cover"? Well, that rule goes out the window when it comes to dating websites! In fact, judging you by your photo is exactly what the sugar baby is going to do!

The photo area on dating websites is the one thing most guys simply fuck up. Of course there is always a tricky balance between privacy and transparency. Sure, you wouldn't want your pictures to be downloaded and spread carelessly around the internet/social media platforms, especially if you're looking to make this arrangement discreet. At the same time, however, you need to show off yourself enough to get some attention from the ladies. A great photo can boost your dating potential, even if your profile is generic or lacks substance.

So what is a good strategy to use? To start off, most sugar dating websites support two types of pictures: public and private. Think of public pictures as your first opportunity to catch her attention. Next, if you decide to upload private photos, be sure to use photos that will set you apart from the rest of her potential sugar daddies.

So you might be thinking, "I don't have any good photos!" Well, there are no excuses in the digital era. Guess what, everyone has a smartphone these days and can take new photos.

Ideally, your public picture should include a close-up and a full body. Not that everything needs to be perfect, but it should show enough of your physical characteristics to draw her attention to your profile. For privacy concerns, you might even choose to blur out your eyes/faces, which is generally acceptable depending on the platform and the website's photo approval guidelines. In other situations, you can also crop your head off of a full body shot that emphasizes your general physique. This photo should simply give a general idea of what you look like without giving away your identity. Remember this: Profiles with at least one public photo will see five to ten times more replies to messages than those without a public photo. Here are some important things to consider when selecting or taking the perfect profile photo:

- Lighting
- Contrast
- Subject (not more than one person in photo)
- Angle
- Posture
- Poor Quality
- Keep the background generic so it doesn't upstage you
- Don't post pics in a dorm room if you're a "millionaire"
- Don't post photos with easily identifiable locations for privacy

In addition to your standard iPhone and Android photo editing abilities, you can download one of several apps to edit your photos:

- Snapseed
- Pixelmator
- FaceTune
- Afterlight
- Adobe Lightroom

Next up is your choice of private photos. This is where things tend to get interesting. Private photos, happily, allow you to control which sugar babies see them. But proceed with caution.

Most men think this is the place to post a bunch of pics in their underwear with a boner. Guess again. Nudes should always be a no-no because they can easily end up in the wrong hands. Nudes may also turn off a potential sugar baby who doesn't necessarily want to get acquainted first by looking at "your meat" - no matter how many inches you are packing, fellas. The safest approach is to be discreet and creative with your private pics. Use this as an opportunity to share a photo of your face and smile or depict preferred interests or activities that might entice a potential sugar baby. Design your private photos to display five main characteristics:

Official

The classic, formal look is never a bad look. Even if you don't need a formal dress code for your line of work, go for it and post a picture in a nice suit from a wedding or another upscale occasion. Just be sure the photo doesn't have ten other groomsmen. Keep it elegant but simple! You can talk all about how classy you are, but nothing says "smart, mature, and distinguished" more than a formal picture. You probably clean it up nicely, so why not let the ladies see?

Lifestyle

This is your more laidback and relaxed photo, one showing you engaging in a hobby you love. Post a photo that shows you at your most genuine, with your face and physique are clearly visible. But be sure the image is taken in an upscale location that backs up your claim as a sugar daddy. That means a photo on your yacht, on the golf course, on the beach showing off your abs, in the gym, or with your feet propped up in a private jet. Let the ladies see evidence of the great lifestyle you have.

Popular

To give the ladies a taste of your charm, popularity, and position in society, post a pic with a group of upscale friends. Make sure that you're the center of attention - and, fer Chrissakes, make sure that you're the best-looking in the group! (You can blur out other people's faces as necessary.) The point is to put your status and wealth on display for the sugar babies to see.

Cultured

If you have a picture of yourself in a unique, artistic setting, this definitely helps in raising curiosity levels of sugar babies. It could be a pic of yourself in a museum, with a celebrity, or a picture of you in an exotic or upscale location most could only dream of. A photo that reflects your cultured background and sense of adventure is the ultimate sugar baby magnet!

Social

This is the more friendly and welcoming picture of you. It should show off a big smile as you pose in front of a nice vibrant background or even with you holding a pet. Girls fucking love puppies! It depicts you as a big sweetheart who loves helpless little things - and it's a scenario that sugar babies simply can't resist. They're thinking of themselves as that little puppy in your arms, after all!

Now, all this advice is just a series of suggestions - but great suggestions. Don't go overboard; no need to go get plastic surgery or buy a dog. But maybe you should get that museum membership or buy that yacht right now. While it's the little things that matter in life, when you're heading for the sugar bowl, it's the big things that matter, as well!

BONUS TIP

Your online profile is one of the most important aspects of sugar dating. It's your key to the city... if you want it. There's so much more to it than you think.

Here's **Additional Tips and Tricks to Making an Outstanding Profile**

http://mysugarguide.com/additional-profile-tips

KEEP YOUR ONLINE SAFETY IN MIND

When using pictures for sugar dating, it's suggested that you don't use the same photos that you use on your other social media platforms. Anyone can do a quick reverse search and track you down on LinkedIn, Instagram, Facebook, etc. And then your private life in the sugar now is ruined, especially if you have a wife in your primary life. As previously mentioned, make sure your public pictures don't contain clues (job, location) that make it easy for someone to identify you.

CHAPTER 7
CHALLENGE

Let's start brainstorming for your ideal online profile. The better your profile looks and sounds, the more likely it's going to be to be sugar baby clickbait. Your job is to find the hottest sugar babies out there, so take this assignment seriously!

Write five ideas for an effective username:

1. ....

2. ....

3. ....

4. ....

5. ....

Write five ideas for your ideal headline:

1. ....

2. ....

3. ....

4. ....

5. ....

This is a good start. I'd recommend do five more of each before you choose. It takes a lot of work to strike gold, but once you do, you will reap the benefits for a long time to come.

MEETING A SUGAR BABY ONLINE: PROFILE DO'S AND DON'TS

When you're using sugar dating platforms to track down your first sugar baby, it's important to have a solid game plan in place. Think of it as starting off a new business or startup. As a CEO, you wouldn't jump in without a solid business plan in place. In fact, you would simply be setting yourself up for failure if you didn't approach this new business venture with a solid strategy.

The same applies to the sugar dating scene. If you don't enter with a solid game plan, you'll find it much harder to achieve the desired outcome in the shortest amount of time. Rather than simply jumping in blind when you create your profile, you should have a solid plan. It's crucial for you to get it right the first time. But where should you begin?.

There are several important profile Do's and Don'ts that you should keep in mind when creating your profile. Whether you are just getting started in sugar dating or you're a seasoned veteran, these Do's and Don'ts are essential for your sanity and survival in the game. The best thing about these tips is they will save you time and frustration and set you up for immediate success. I told you this book was a wise investment! Ready? Let's go!

PROFILE DOs

Let's start with what you should do to ensure sugar bowl success. When creating your profile, here are essential Do's to follow regardless, of the platform you choose to use.

DO give yourself proper time to craft a well-written profile

While you may be looking to join the sugar dating scene primarily for fun, it doesn't mean that you shouldn't take writing your profile very seriously. In fact, you will be judged by what you write. Keep in mind that spelling is of the utmost importance and you should always use a word editor to ensure proper spelling and grammar. Poor spelling and grammar place you in a bad light and can be a major turn-off to potential sugar babies. Remember that your profile provides sugar babies with the most obvious first impression of you. It's like your business card. It tells your story to new people. If you want to attract the right sugar baby, you need to spend time creating the best first impression of yourself. So when writing your profile, don't rush it. Take your time. Read it aloud - two or three times - and always, always, always spellcheck and proofread before publishing.

Be sure to familiarize yourself with the dating site and its community guidelines. Next, think about how you want to portray yourself to potential sugar babies, as well as what you might expect in return. Once you have your intentions straight, you can begin crafting the perfect profile. Remember that every word you write counts and will play a role in how sugar babies perceive you. Make sure you include some good conversation points in your profile, including:

- Hobbies and interests
- Goals related to sugar dating
- Why you're on the site
- Personal preferences, such as favorite music and food
- Upcoming travel destinations or events

Basically, you want to design your profile information as a set of conversation starters. It's an invitation to sugar babies to communicate with you. Here's an example of a brief, yet very insightful, profile description:

I'm looking for a beautiful, smart, sugar baby to join me for fun and exciting adventures. I am not looking for anything too serious, as I am recently divorced with no kids. In my ideal arrangement, we would meet up twice a week. While beauty is important to me, I am seeking a nice balance between sexiness and intelligence. Model quality looks are a plus, combined with the ability to share intellectual conversations. A mental connection is just as important as physical appearance for me. As a business owner with a flexible schedule, I am open to relaxing nights at home, fine dining around town, or spontaneous vacations to destinations of your dreams, from the warm Caribbean Islands to the Rocky Mountains. Message

me and let me know why you think we are a good match.
Perhaps we can explore a deeper connection together.

This brief example is easy to read, filled with good information, and effectively tells two sides of the story: what you're looking for, as well as what she can expect from you.

DO present an ideal image of yourself

You may think that sugar babies simply want gifts and money, but they also pay close attention to your physical appearance. They will notice small details you include in photos and in your profile content. They are looking for clues - so make sure you share the best ones that flatter you the most. On the other hand, some sugar babies are simply more attracted to looks than others. In fact, there are those who simply want a no-strings-attached, discreet arrangement with a mature and wealthy man who can spoil them.

If this is the kind of sugar baby you want, you better make sure your public pictures present you in this favorable light that emphasizes your physical appearance.

DO state your expectations clearly.

It all comes back to your profile description. Before you even write it, you should already know what you want and what you expect in return. Then you can work on turning thoughts into words and express your intentions in a clear and concise manner. You don't have to be a professional writer to get this done correctly. Use short and well-punctuated sentences to tell your story - or even bullet points that express everything that is important to you. (Refer to the description example posted in the "How to Create a Profile" section).

> It's amazing how many men can screw up something so easy.
>
> *Here's* **10 Biggest Profile Mistakes Men Make**
>
> **http://mysugarguide.com/profile-mistakes**

BONUS TIP

PROFILE DON'TS

Now that you know what you need to do to get started on the sugar dating websites, it is also important to know what you shouldn't do. Here are some crucial don'ts to heed while you start writing your profile. They will keep you from attracting the wrong prospects. They will also remind you of certain bounds of decency that you need to follow, so that you can prevent your profile from being banned.

DON'T have unrealistic expectations

A common mistake new sugar daddies make is to expect a high-class sugar baby while they're only willing to offer minimal allowance or value in exchange. If you're on a budget, don't make false promises in your profile. And don't get caught up in chasing sugar babies out of your league. Stick to realistic expectations as to whom you expect to meet. Unrealistic expectations waste both your time and hers. It does not mean you should eliminate model-quality sugar babies. You can still pursue them, but just don't invest too much time if you are not getting favorable responses.

Never ever be a cheap ass, liar or come off as overly desperate! Set expectations clearly on your profile and use the appropriate advanced search filters. And if you're still struggling with your income and don't truly have sugar daddy status in your bank account, then take a breather. Back off and build up a genuine bankroll before you jump into the sugar dating scene. No one likes a faker in the sugar bowl and poseurs are easily found out.

DON'T be overly secretive

We're certainly not suggesting that you should be a 100% open book when offering details about yourself and what you wish to get out of sugar dating. But you don't need to act like you work for the National Security Agency either.

You can be open about many things without giving away important aspects of your personal life. For example, you can state what kind of sugar baby you like, your sex life preferences, what your hobbies are, and whether you're single, married, or divorced. It's never a bad idea to keep the personal details about your life private. Below are some of the common pieces of information that you might want to keep a bit closer to the chest and not share on your profile with the sugar baby community:

- Employer or company you own
- Income
- Full legal name
- Social media accounts
- Home or work address
- Private details about other sugar babies
- Family details (about your wife, kids or ex)
- Relationship or family issues

It's a good idea to be upfront about whether or not you're married. Face it, some sugar babies don't want the drama of being with a married guy. While this might eliminate some potential sugar babies from your pool, that's a better strategy. Take it from Jerry Bigs. Because if you hide your marital status from her now, and she finds out later, things can go really wrong. (On the other hand, some sugar babies prefer married men and actively avoid the ones who are single or divorced, as married men tend to be less clingy.)

A married sugar daddy means the relationship comes with built-in boundaries, which can be very appealing. She knows you're far less likely to try to turn the arrangement into a more serious relationship than what she's looking for, or even ask her to run away and get married, because you already have someone who requires the majority of your time.

Either way, disclosing your relationship status in your profile allows potential sugar babies to filter men based on their preferences, so that the ones who are interested can come to you, and you don't have to waste your time with the ones who aren't. In some cases, married men choose to protect their privacy by stating that they are single in their profile and then will reveal the truth in a later conversation.

Whatever you do and don't decide to disclose, remember when it comes to personal information, less is more.

DON'T use a username that can be linked to your social media

Nowadays, your family, friends, and colleagues use social media in many different ways. You certainly don't want your sugar daddy profile to be linked back to your social media accounts (Facebook, SnapChat, Instagram, etc.). Obviously, it's never a good idea to use your real name as a part of your username. Make sure your username is unique and distinct. Make it such that it's not easily traceable back to you. If you really want to be discrete, you should register using a throwaway email address. This will further ensure none of your sugar life can be linked back to your primary life.

DON'T get banned

It is always a good idea to understand the community guidelines of the sugar community in which you are participating. Every platform has strict rules to ensure the safety of their members. It is a good practice to refrain from any mention of financial compensation or pay-per-meet etc. There should be no mention of money for sex in your profile. Don't be stupid.

CHAPTER 8
CHALLENGE

This book is not only about getting to know sugar babies. It's a way to have you get to know **you** before you venture into the sugar bowl. Let's help you find out more about you. Again, the more interesting you make your profile, the better your chances will be to meeting the girl of your dreams. These women get dozens upon dozens of messages from guys just like you. Distinguish yourself with an extra bit of imagination. Stick out and make yourself *more interesting:*

List five of your favorite hobbies (bonus points if they're not sports or cars):

1. ....

2. ....

3. ....

4. ....

5. ....

List five interesting things about you that no one knows:

1. ....

2. ....

3. ....

4. ....

5. ....

List five personal things about you that you promise never to include in your online profile:

1. ....

2. ....

3. ....

4. ....

5. ....

THE FIRST COMMUNICATION

very sugar dating platform approaches messaging quite different. But there are some consistencies. In most cases you need to have a paid account in order to send or receive messages. Be sure to upgrade your account as this is a critical step in order to close the deal with your potential sugar baby. Now that you have upgraded your account and your sugar dating profile is now complete, it's time to dive deeper into the sugar bowl.

The first step is to start sending and receive messages! Your first communication will be very important for the future of your sugar dating. First impressions matter, and they will determine which babies you end up with. As I have said before, the sugar bowl community is a tight one, and news about good impressions travels fast. News about bad impressions travel even faster - and could freeze you out of the scene. Even if the ratio is in your favor, and there are plenty of sugar babies to go around, you can easily turn off many sugar babies by sending the wrong messages. So how should you kick things off?

THE SECRETS TO STARTING A CONVERSATION: YOUR MESSAGING STRATEGY

As a sugar daddy, the ball is in your court. But you have to work at it. Don't expect a flood of messages from potential sugar babies that magically meet your desired criteria. It simply won't happen this way. Sugar babies receive a lot of messages, far more than the average sugar daddy on the platform. As you can imagine, the messages range from kinky and bizarre to bland and extravagant. You need to stand out from the pack. The best way is to be unique and get straight to the point, charmingly so, of course.

If you have been heeding the sage wisdom of your very own Jerry Bigs - and why wouldn't you? - by now you have learned to properly choose an interesting public profile and clever username.

Just to be sure, you might want to go back and revisit these sections to make sure you're up to speed. Your romantic future is at stake; you will need everything in your arsenal to come together and work in perfect harmony. That way, you can effectively grab her attention.

That sweet sugar baby you're crushing on online probably has an inbox flooded with lame messages or indecent proposals. You don't want to pile on top of that crap with some message that's equally lame or indecent. Do you? I didn't think so. So now's your chance to shine and distinguish yourself from the other armature daddies.

Invest serious time and ingenuity in your initial message. Make sure it is original and not just a "copy paste" essay. You want it to be casual and fun, and intriguing enough to prompt a response from that special woman. The message should express what you liked about her profile, why she stood out to you, and what you're looking for.

TIPS FOR YOUR FIRST MESSAGE

- Keep it short and sweet.
- Get hints for wording from her "about me" or "interested in" section. Find something meaningful to say regarding one or two of her interests or other profile highlights that stand out. It will make you come off as thoughtful, helping you to establish a connection.
- Offer a brief description of what you can do for her.
- Refrain from using internet slang such as "luv" "ur" "ya", "wyd", etc.
- Avoid spelling mistakes in your first message.
- Avoid writing in ALL CAPS.
- It's best to not mention sexual desires in your initial message; save this conversation for a private text message off the platform or in person.

Let's look at this sample sugar baby profile. It's a good example of an initial message you could make to this sugar baby.

"Successful" and "attractive" are words most women might use to describe me. And it seems I may have finally met my match. I just shared my private photos and will let you be the judge. I am not here to waste your time as you seem to be a busy professional and know exactly what you are looking for. That makes two of us. Since we both can appreciate time, and love to travel, I would love to get to know you. Perhaps over a brunch at the Four Seasons this weekend, where we can compare passport stamps?

Some people without a knack for words like to copy and paste a generic message template for all the sugar babies. This is referred to as the "spray and pray" method. It doesn't really involve much ingenuity; it's a numbers game. But sometimes this can work in your favor. Jerry Bigs still recommends the personal touch.

Don't be afraid to contact as many sugar babies as you can during the duration of your paid membership. At the same time, remember that a lot of sugar babies on the sites know and talk to one another. If you're giving all of them the same generic message, then it's just a matter of time before they start to catch on. So to keep your credibility intact, I recommend that you change it up occasionally. Keep your personal message unique. See how the ladies respond. They will tell you which sections of your message really moved them, so you will know what parts to keep and what parts to change as you keep refining your message. Eventually, based on your message response rate, you will find your sweet spot.

My advice is to start with your basic message, but go one step further. Tweak it and personalize it just enough for each girl. You can accomplish this by adding an opening line about how you read their profile. Briefly quote the part of the profile that caught your attention. This won't tax your creative imagination, but it will be enough to personalize your copy and paste template and grab a sugar baby's attention.

BONUS TIP

Sugar Babies will judge your profile. They sort through dozens of messages a day. So will yours stand out from the others?

Here's **Confessions of a Sugar Baby: Their Ideal Profile**

http://mysugarguide.com/ideal-profile

YOU GOT MAIL: LET THE GAMES BEGIN

After sending a few messages and getting your feet wet, it's only a matter of time before you get an actual reply from your prospective sugar baby. Don't be discouraged if you do not get a reply right away as not all members are checking the site every hour like their work email. In some cases, you might get a reply several weeks later.

When you finally get a reply from a sugar baby, here's another helpful Jerry Bigs tip: Ask your potential sugar baby to continue the conversation via text message. Moving the message from the dating platform is always a good idea as it allows for more fluid conversations. Plus, you can choose to share more photos or videos of yourself. It is always suggested (especially for those who wish to be more discreet) to avoid sharing your real phone number. There are lots of texting apps that provide anonymous numbers for you to maintain privacy. Below are some apps you can download from the app store to create a second phone number. Some apps require a phone number in order to use them, like Whatsapp and telegram. Check out the following apps and find one that works best for you:

iPlum

$4.99/month: second phone number, calling & texting app with voicemail, no ads, complete privacy, cancel anytime, no contracts.

Google Voice

Free: second phone number, allows for voice and text and picture messaging.

Confide

Free: use your Google voice number to register, allows for truly end- to-end encrypted picture and text messaging in addition to a screenshot blocking feature.

Telegram

Free: use your Google voice number to register, allows for voice and text and picture messaging.

Snapchat

Free: use your Google voice number to register, allows for voice and video and text and picture messaging.

WhatsApp

Free: use your Google voice number to register, allows for voice and text and picture messaging.

Sideline

Paid: second phone number, allows for voice and text and picture messaging.

Hushed

Paid: second phone number, allows for voice and text and picture messaging.

Skype

Free: register a new user account. So that you don't mix business and pleasure.

Kik

No phone number needed, not as convenient as WhatsApp, Telegram, Google Voice, or Skype

LET'S TRADE SOME PICS

Like you, most sugar babies also want to maintain some sort of privacy online. Some decide to post the minimal number of public pictures on their profile for you to view. Once you have exchanged numbers and have started to message one another, you may want to see more pictures. How should you go about asking?

It's simple; just ask. Courteously. Alternately, you can ask if she has an Instagram account you can follow. This is a normal request, not a pushy one, and it will help you get a clearer picture of her physical appearance. Just be prepared to share some additional photos of your own in exchange . This is not the time and place to ask for nudes, as this will most quickly kill the vibe and turn her away.

ARRANGING FOR THE FIRST VIDEO SKYPE OR FACETIME MEETING

It's a good sugar daddy strategy to arrange for a virtual face-to-face meeting before the first physical meeting. This is a great time saver. After all, we've all been on the awkward first date which goes south fast because she's thirty pounds heavier than you expected. With Skype, you'll be able to see each other clearly, uncover hidden body features, and show off that beautiful smile. FaceTime and WhatsApp are also common options to use, and you can arrange for a quick (10-15-minute) video call that works best for both of you.

Avoid using this live video session to share any nudes or expose parts of your body. It's just tacky and shows a lack of polish on your end. Besides offending the lady, you may screw yourself up; the worst-case scenario is that some unscrupulous sugar baby could record the whole naked thing just to later use it against you.

While we're at it, avoid the temptation of sending unsolicited dick pics, as a general rule. Most girls tend to find it creepy and gross. If you're going to exchange nudes, wait until you've both gotten to know and trust each other better, and make sure it's something she will appreciate. If you're going to send them, you better make sure to get some in return.

Use this video meeting as an opportunity to gauge how well you vibe and whether you share the same intentions. Be sure to express what you expect from her up front and give her the chance to say what she is looking for in the arrangement. This video meeting could be just enough to break the ice and help her to feel more comfortable, paving the way for a meeting face to face.

CHAPTER 9
CHALLENGE

That first message is super critical. Think of it like a first impression at a networking meeting, or your pick-up line at a bar when approaching a girl (remember the old fashioned way?). The most important thing is to take interest in the women you're messaging, refer to some of her interests as laid out in her profile, and remember to share some cool facts about yourself while messaging. Be relatable. Obviously that's a tough thing to do without seeing a girl. So try this:

Go back to your Chapter 8 Challenge. Pick one of your hobbies and imagine your ideal sugar baby just listed it as one of her favorite hobbies.

Now, write a three-to-five sentence message to her. Accentuate what you have in common. Tell her how this hobby enriches your life. Ask what it has done for her life. Be upbeat, illuminating, and show extreme interest in what she has to say.

....

....

....

....

....

Great! That's how you're going to get the best replies. In this case, saying "Hey, what's up?" is not going to work. Present yourself as an interesting dude who finds her interesting, then watch the magic happen!

Now that you've messaged a sugar baby who has caught your eye, and she has enthusiastically messaged back, it's time to take it to the next level. Meeting in person.

ARRANGING THE FIRST PHYSICAL MEETING

ongratulations! You must have done everything until now. Because you have made it to this stage of conversation. It's safe to assume that you have crafted a clever and intriguing profile, defined your expectations, messaged some sugar babies, exchanged phone numbers, traded some photos, and now it has come time to finally meet in person.

Meeting each other in person is a big step.

This is where the arrangement is ready to take shape. Not all sugar babies are wired the same. While most platforms discourage any sort of PPM or pay-per-meet, some sugar babies might simply require this in exchange for her time. This is where you have to remember to stick to your budget and use negotiation skills. The objective is to make sure you don't get stuck in the habit of repeatedly handing over money to get a sugar baby to agree to a face-to-face meeting. Here are some techniques you might consider in an effort to defuse a coffee shop pay-per-meet request.

- Let her know you are happy to cover her food, drinks, gas, tolls, or her Uber charges both ways. Assure you that if you mutually decide to move forward with a date, you are a very generous guy and are willing to take care of her needs.
- Be upfront and tell her you don't pay to meet. But if she agrees to meet in person, you are prepared to cover all expenses.

You may have briefly discussed online what you both expect out of this relationship. However, your first meeting is the best chance to clearly express your expectations. Don't be afraid to discuss your sexual expectations with her. Face-to-face conversations are always more meaningful and they allow you to communicate in more than just words. You can both read each other's nonverbal cues in this setting, such as body language, tone, eye contact, touch, etc. This is the best time to express to your sugar baby what you really want and what you're willing to offer in return. Ready to get started? Here are some useful tips.

Schedule the first meeting in a public place

It's always a good idea to arrange for the first meeting in a public place. It should be open enough so that you'll both be comfortable, but quiet enough to allow you to have a private conversation. The more comfortable you are, the quicker you can break the ice and get down to business.

A coffee shop is a great option. It's comfortable, convenient, and you can easily bail within a half-hour if things don't work out. Dinner is typically a popular option, but you may be stuck there for hours if the two of you don't hit it off. And that can be miserable. Another meeting option could be at your local pub/bar, where you can both feel comfortable in a small crowd, and you can unwind over a drink or two. Or make a hasty getaway, if needed.

The first date: Getting it right the first time

Once you're ready to meet your sugar baby, the top priority is to make her feel at ease. This is why getting to know her in advance over text and video chat can help ease this initial tension. Since you are in a public place, be sure to walk up and greet her just as you would an old friend. Decide when you see her whether she would welcome a polite handshake or a warm hug.

Do you like what you see? Of course, you do! Be sure to give her a sincere compliment on her looks, eyes, body, hair, nails, or outfit. This is an indicator to her that you approve of her in person and immediately and strategically sets a nice relaxed tone. Since you have already conversed online, be sure to skip the bland small talk. Instead, jump into some fun ice-breaker questions which allow you to get to know more about one another.

Be sure to be prepared to share info about yourself as well so it doesn't feel like a rapid-fire interview. Make sure the chat goes both ways. Before this meeting, hopefully you memorized some of your potential sugar baby's interests. All of this could be gleaned easily from several sources: her profile, her emails, and your online chats. You're not starting from scratch here; you already know what she is into. This makes for a more fluid conversation in person. Here are some great questions you can ask on your first date:

- Are you currently working? What type of work do you do?
- Are you still in school? What did/do you study?
- What types of music do you enjoy?
- Did you grow up here? Where are you originally from?
- Do you drink? Do you party or do drugs?
- What was your favorite place you have traveled?
- Have you had an arrangement before? What kind? Why did it end?

- What was your longest sugar dating arrangement?

When the time is appropriate, your conversation needs to be able to turn from your favorite chef to your wildest sexual fantasies.

The big question is, "How do I get there?"

Since you are reading this Jerry Bigs book, and you are already finding it a godsend, we will assume you are a confident, charismatic sugar daddy. You're a guy who knows how to make his sugar baby feel extremely confident about herself. You can do this by giving her a sexual compliment. This way, you've pivoted the conversation strategically from the casual to the erotic.

Your sugar baby will feel excited to be interacting with you because of the sense of mutual attraction. Be blunt and to the point. After all, you should be confident by now that she's into you, so go ahead and tell her that you find her sexy.

BONUS TIP

Discretion is important, but you never want to make it seem like you're lying or keeping information from your sugar baby. It will simply make her uncomfortable.

Here's **10 Questions Your Sugar Baby Will Ask and How to Reply**

http://mysugarguide.com/questions-to-answer

It's always a nervous experience, meeting someone for the first time. Especially if one or both of you are new to sugar relationships. The key is to focus on getting to know each other and seeing if this is the right arrangement for both of you.

She is not that into you

You have been with her over an hour, but there's little energy to the exchange. Maybe she's communicating almost exclusively in one-word answers. Or she takes what seems like hours in between responses. You've tried opening her up with open-ended, meaningful questions, but it's just not happening.

Communication is a two-way street. Maybe she's just that nervous, maybe she's just really dull in person - or maybe the connection just isn't there. Either way, it's time to cut your losses and move on. There's plenty of fish in the sea and you don't need to waste a bunch of time trying to force a particular arrangement to work.

CHAPTER 10
CHALLENGE

It's crazy, but true: The easiest way to get someone to like you is to talk about *them*, not blather about yourself! Ask good questions, listen, and then ask more questions! A sugar daddy is more likely to hook someone if you're a good listener. Smart and caring questions lead to more questions. And that leads to more good things... both vertically and horizontally.

Write out five questions you would want to ask your ideal sugar baby that emphasize her, not you:

1. ....

2. ....

3. ....

4. ....

5. ....

Great. Think of questions like these as aces up your sleeve in a hot card game. And the more good questions you have, the better the chances you have at winning the pot.

But before you win, there's some important Dos and Don'ts to remember...

COMMON DOs AND DON'Ts FOR SUGAR DADDIES

You're making progress, reader - and you are learning some important lessons in how to work the sugar bowl.

We have gone from why you would want to be a sugar daddy to finding your first sugar baby. Now that you have gained a world of knowledge about this new form of modern dating, you may be ready to take the plunge and jump into your first arrangement. Whether you're just getting started in the game, a seasoned veteran or coming out of "sugar retirement", there are certain golden rules you need to be aware of prior to your first date.

Let's start with some common Dos and Don'ts.

DOs

DO be transparent regarding time commitments

Now is the best time to be open and honest with yourself - and with her - regarding how much time you're willing to commit to this arrangement. Remember that your sugar baby also has her own life, so how do you balance between the two? Of course, since you had the chance to first meet your sugar baby online, you may have already set out general expectations regarding time commitments. However, these still need to be ironed out when you meet in person. You may have both said you want to meet twice a month. But now that you're face-to-face, it's a good time to get real: discuss the logistics of how, when and where to meet. Or better yet, ask if you both still feel the same way about the earlier plan?

Take advantage of your face-to-face meeting to express what you both want out of the arrangement. Discussion requires compromise, so you can tell soon enough whether she's flexible or rigid. Whether she will meet you halfway. Or whether it's her way or the highway.

And flexibility is key. Your schedules will not always overlap as easily as you may think. For example, what happens when you need to call off a meeting? What happens if something comes up on her end? You should both be considerate of one another's time, and be gracious and considerate to alert the other when there are last-minute changes in plans. Or be kind enough to accept a postponement without drama. Maybe a little disappointment, but not a scolding.

Remember that it's not a bad thing if you both can't agree on everything. If it's something you're not willing to compromise, don't be afraid to stand your ground. Remember that you're now in an arrangement that is out of the norm. Don't kick back to traditional dating mode, where you have to compromise everything to the point of personal inconvenience.

In sugar dating, it's all about meeting someone who fits with your expectations. Some sugar babies are experts at negotiating, especially if she's had a few previous arrangements. Be careful not to give too much power by bending too far backwards. Because a shrewd and seasoned (and manipulative) sugar baby will pick up on this behavior. Then what? It will end up costing you big-time in the long run.

DO be prepared to spoil your sugar baby when she deserves it

Despite all of your budgeting and managing expectations, your sugar baby will still expect you to spoil her. Your mindset from the beginning should be to prepare to spoil her according to your financial abilities. Don't be afraid to be generous, but make sure to be consistent. If you spent $200 on your first dinner date, be prepared to spoil her with dinners of a similar caliber moving forward. The first date is where you get a chance to set the bar for her expectations.

You should never force your sugar baby to come begging for gifts or cash. You should always maintain your half of the arrangement. After you initially set expectations for the relationship, agreed on a budget, and agreed on the frequency of meetings, be sure to keep your word. Consistency is key.

Inconsistency is not an option. In fact, it's the fastest way to ruin your reputation with sugar babies, especially in your hometown. You may not be familiar with her personal goals and financial situation, but she may be relying on the regular allowance you give her to help with things like her rent payment. Skipping just one allowance period may put her in an uncomfortable situation. Keep your end of the bargain and make sure she doesn't get frustrated by having to ask you for the standard gifts you started out giving. Honor your end of the agreement. If you keep flaking out, you will find your sugar baby doing a disappearing act. She will start looking elsewhere for a sugar daddy - and your name will be mud in the sugar bowl.

DO appear presentable whenever you meet your sugar baby

It may sound out of place to remind a grown and cultured gentleman such as you to practice basic hygiene. However, you'd be surprised at how many gentlemen forget some simple grooming tips - and that will be a complete turn-off for the sugar baby. For example, you may be used to getting away with a five o'clock shadow, messy hair, or the occasional wrinkled and stained shirt.

While your wife or other women your age may have grown used to these shortcomings after years of marriage, younger ladies tend to be very picky. They will notice the lack of hygiene or self-care from a mile away. You have spent all this time wooing a sexy sugar baby online and meeting her for the first date. It would be a shame after all this hard work to sabotage future dates with your ideal sugar baby because of some basic hygiene issues, so make sure you practice a few basics:

- Make sure your face is shaved or your facial hair neatly trimmed.
- Avoid the scruffy look, unless it matches your photos.
- For subsequent visits with your sugar baby, manscape below the waist and trim your pubes before each and every date.
- Unless you're full-on European, then consider showering and using deodorant before every sugar baby date. (If she likes your manly funk, adjust accordingly.)

BONUS TIP

Sugar Babies have some triggers that either tell them to stay or leave. Here's help identifying those.

Here's **Confessions of a Sugar Baby: Will They Keep You or Dump You?**

http://mysugarguide.com/sugar-baby-triggers

DON'TS

Similar to the importance of practicing some good habits, there are also some things you should be sure *not* to do. Understanding these common no-no's will ensure that you don't embarrass yourself, or even worse, completely blow it with your potential sugar baby.

DON'T assume your sugar baby wants to fuck on the first date

So you're excited about meeting your sugar baby for the first time. You've showered, shaved, manscaped, made dinner reservations, and even bought a small gift for your sugar baby. You've re-read appropriate sections of this book about first meeting behavior and conversation. So you're good to go, my man.

You arrive early, you're excited, and you're ready for what's ahead. A few minutes later, she walks in. Your heart beats fast and you instantly get a boner. She's hot as fuck. Hell, she even looks better than in her pictures! Like any normal guy, you immediately start calculating scenarios in your head. What if? Could I get lucky tonight? Is she into me? Does she suck dick? But then after dinner, some great conversation, and agreeing to a sugar daddy-sugar baby arrangement, she announces that she has to go home.

What the fuck went wrong?

Take a deep breath and don't lose your shit. Stick with Jerry Bigs and I'll explain what's happening here.

Understandably, you're disappointed. Perhaps even shocked and upset. But remember that most sugar dates don't end up horizontal on the very first date. The first date is what's known in the sugar bowl as a M&G: Meet and Greet. It's your chance to break the ice, get acquainted, and iron out the technical details for your future arrangement.

Sometimes, but not always, payment isn't expected for the M&G. Which is why sex isn't part of this encounter. It's simply a trial run, to see if you both vibe with one another. And even if everything goes perfect, sex still might not be something she is willing to consider under the circumstances of an initial M&G.

Even if she feels comfortable with you - and she does, since she just agreed to an arrangement, fer Chrissakes - she might not be ready to host you at her place. And it's too early in the relationship for her to trust you enough to follow you to yours. If you're going to a nice hotel, you should have made the reservation in advance. But if you're making the reservation without asking if she wants to have sex on the first date, then you're being presumptuous. Presumers set themselves up for disappointment in the form of a non-refundable room cancellation - and no pussy.

Bottom line: Good things cum to - and on - those who wait!

In the end, it all comes down to prep work and strong communication. It's about your previous conversations leading up to the M&G, your ability to charm her, and the money! (Did I mention the money?)

If you have discussed in advance the possibility of sex on the first date with your sugar baby, and she agrees, then go for it! In fact, you'll often find that many college girls will happily give it up because they are blown away by your wealth, social status, and charm. Offer her what she likes, negotiate with her responsibly about your expectations - and then give her a sugar daddy fucking she won't forget!

DON'T be too demanding or controlling

While you're paying for everything, keep things in perspective and don't let the power trip go to your head. Some sugar daddies are used to being in control of all aspects of their lives. You may be a CEO, doctor, or an executive. You spend a good portion of your day giving orders. However, you should try to separate this bossy persona in your primary life from the persona in your sugar dating life. Your sugar baby is not your employee. Talk to her as an equal, not someone on the payroll. Respect is earned, not given.

Unless you are in a Dom/Sub relationship, you should avoid this controlling mentality. Or learn to tone it down on the dating scene. In the sugar bowl, the goal is to establish give-and-take arrangements where the power dynamic is theoretically around 50-50. You should work together to find mutual ground. She has something to bring to the table, and you also have something to offer in return. She offers far more than just sex, and you offer her things money can't buy. Treat people the way you want to be treated. Or even better.

DON'T talk too much about your personal drama

Everyone needs someone to talk to when times are tough. Having someone to listen to your personal problems is the best way to relieve stress. At some point during the course of your relationship, you may find yourself caught up in some bullshit. It may come from your family, work, friends. Whenever you meet with your sugar baby, this can seem like the perfect forum to get it all off your chest. It's only natural, primarily because your sugar baby may make you feel at ease, happy, and comfortable.

You may feel tempted to talk about personal topics such as:

- Wife and kids' issues
- Previous sugar baby drama
- Potential lawsuits you're facing
- Client payment complications
- Health issues

Even if your sugar baby relationship is firing on all cylinders, even if you feel she really gets you - STOP! Jerry Bigs has some crucial advice: you should simply avoid these whining sessions all together. Even if she smiles and nods compassionately, she really doesn't give a shit about your drama or work issues. In fact, the words "my wife" and "my kids" might make her cringe. And it's just bad strategy to talk about your financial headaches - since this will make her go looking for a sugar daddy with more stable earnings!

Overall, it is best to avoid these topics all together, especially if you are trying to keep your primary life private. While your sugar baby may seem like the perfect listener, don't get into the habit of constantly complaining about your personal life. Remember that she also has her own life and her own set of problems. Your issues are most likely far more complex and on a much larger scale. But guess what? Her concerns about her negative bank account and her flat tire are more important to her than your lawsuit and work problems.

The contractors remodeling your house are incompetent and behind schedule? She's living in a tiny apartment with roommates, her landlord won't fix the A/C in the middle of summer, and she might be a couple of rent payments away from an eviction notice.

Bottom line: Learn to spend your time with your sugar baby more constructively. She's your getaway with reality - so don't drag her into your private hell. Quit your bitching and complaining. Instead, focus on having fun. Because after a while, she's going to ghost you and find a daddy with more positive big dick energy and who has his proverbial shit together.

Here are some more time-tested, field-approved Jerry Bigs tips on how to guarantee having a great date with your fabulous sugar baby:

DON'T be overly braggadocious

To impress our sugar babies, some of us make the misstep of talking ourselves up too much. That ends up sounding like bragging and it's not sexy. Men, this is how we are wired: We tend to like ourselves too much. We can't get enough of our accomplishments, our future goals, and being self-centered. It's a variation on locker room talk. And the louder the bragging, the more insecure you probably are. Make a note of it - and stuff a sock in it, fellas. Be simple, humble, and honest if you want to get her attention, especially on the first date. And keep it up on every date after that. These sugar babies don't want drama - unless it's between the sheets!

The best approach is to show her that you are indeed who you say you are, without overdoing it. Lean more in the direction of the humblebrag. Casually share photos that showcase you in a location that would be considered exclusive, hanging with VIPs. The idea is to non-verbally show her that you're someone special. That's far more effective than sounding like an egomaniac with deep pockets.

Why should you reel it in? Because less is more. A smart sugar baby knows that guys who spend all their time talking about their wealth usually don't have as much money as they suggest. She is aware that flashy cars can be leased and the penthouse can be rented. If you brag too much, she may start looking for clues that you are simply too good to be true. And then you have a skeptical sugar baby on your hands - someone who is eyeing the exit door. She wants a bona fide sugar daddy - not a secret salt daddy struggling to maintain his false persona.

Sometimes a flashy sugar daddy can also tip off a sugar baby about some disconnect. Think on this: The majority of sugar daddies with unlimited disposable income didn't get to that point by making reckless, extravagant purchases. They have an above-average residence in a nice part of town and might even drive a Tesla, but they still count their nickels and dimes cautiously and don't go on crazy spending sprees. They have wise fiscal priorities. And the savvy sugar baby knows this. She doesn't need to hear constant bragging; so long as you keep picking up the check and keep the gifts coming, she really doesn't care about the rest.

CHAPTER 11
CHALLENGE

If you want to be a good sugar daddy and keep your babies coming around, you need to take these Dos and Don'ts seriously. You will absolutely find yourself in a better position every time if you follow these. This next challenge is a serious reminder that too many don'ts in the sugar bowl will guarantee you find yourself baby-less and alone.

Make the commitment to yourself and re-write these sentences:

I will be transparent regarding time commitments.

....

I will be prepared to spoil my sugar baby when she deserves it.

....

I will appear presentable whenever I meet my sugar baby.

....

I will not always assume my sugar baby wants to fuck on the first date.

....

I will not be too demanding or controlling.

....

I will not talk too much about my personal drama.

....

I will not be overly braggadocious.

....

Again, all of this is for your own good, brother. It's about keeping you and your sugar baby happy. When you bring a smile to her sweet face, then you're also going to be very happy. Want to know more? Then keep reading.

12.

HOW TO KEEP YOUR SUGAR BABY HAPPY

You've undertaken a thoughtful search online. You've sent smart and entertaining messages. You've been honest, but not overshared. And your dates have been warm, friendly, and chatty.

Since you have followed all these Jerry Bigs tips to the letter, you will eventually find a sugar baby whom you simply can't get enough of. Lucky dog! Pat yourself on the back. You're a sugar daddy success story in the making.

I don't mean to piss on your parade... but it's important not to fall into the trap of becoming overly comfortable. Complacency is a huge problem in all relationships - especially in sugar dating. Fortunately, sugar relationships do not follow the same rules as traditional dating. There is lots of wiggle room in these non-traditional arrangements.

Regardless of the leeway, you constantly need to put in effort in order to keep the arrangement exciting. It takes constant thoughtfulness to keep your sugar baby satisfied.

This extends beyond fancy dinners, wild sex, and a generous allowance. You need to do everything you can to keep things fresh and interesting. Be sure to set some goals or bucket list items the both of you can look forward to as you work towards these relationship milestones. You should also pay close attention to what makes her tick. What is her favorite music? Favorite candy? Favorite flower? Favorite gemstone? Favorite clothes designer? Favorite restaurant? Keep a list of these items as they come up in casual conversation. And dip into these surefire happiness starters from time to time, especially if things seem to be slowing down. It's the little things that will spice things up and keep her around for a long time.

A happy sugar baby should be a fun and energetic young girl. It's important to keep her happy - because that upbeat energy will enhance the arrangement. And you'll be a lot happier, as well. We're not saying that you need to go overboard as you would in a typical relationship, but there are certain things you can do to keep things fresh. Luckily, I just happen to have a sure-fire list of tactics that will keep the smile on her face, that spring in her step, and that ongoing fire in your bedsheets.

START BY HONORING YOUR OBLIGATIONS

The most important thing is to start with the basics. If you don't live up to your end of the arrangement with your sugar baby, this is a sure way to get her upset and cause conflict. The most common example is when men fail to honor their agreements in terms of financial expectations. If you have agreed to give her an allowance of $5,000 a month, you should be prepared to honor that each and every month moving forward.

Remember that when you're helping your sugar baby financially, you are a key part of her income. She has most likely tightly planned her budget around these monthly funds. So if haven't paid her allowance for the past two weeks, expect all hell to break loose - and rightfully so. You can't expect her to answer your text and happily meet up with you when you have thrown off her finances, or the landlord is hounding her. If you want to keep this relationship humming, then you need to avoid making too many empty promise$ that you can't keep.

Until you have established a clear line of trust, you should never pay her upfront in advance for the month. In some cases, it could be a scam. Some shady sugar babies will simply "go dark" on you and move along to the next victim willing to line her pockets like a chump.

Honoring obligations is also about keeping promises about dates. And then making sure you arrive on time. The best way of avoiding unnecessary stress within the arrangement is by keeping an open schedule. There are, admittedly, some younger sugar babies who become aggressively flaky about making plans to meet - or about arriving on time. So you should be able to adjust your plans and remain as flexible as possible - within reason. Unless she is delusional and has unrealistic expectations from you, most sugar babies will be quite happy if you honor all the promised obligations of your arrangement.

KEEP AN OPEN MIND

In the sugar dating scene, many of the conventional rules of a traditional relationship simply don't apply. When you're planning to jump into the sugar bowl, it's best to enter this type of arrangement by unlearning old rules. Sugar daddies should forget about the traditional girlfriend-boyfriend mentality that was instilled in you since you were young.

Sugar babies are mostly younger ladies who can be sexy, self-absorbed, materialistic, and sometimes freaky. They can teach an old dog new tricks. Don't fight the lessons; accept the new and exciting ways to explore things you haven't experienced before, both in and out of the bedroom. Think of this as a unique opportunity to go to new places, to try what you've never done before, and most importantly, to get out of your comfort zone.

Depending on your budget and availability with your sugar baby, an open mind will keep both of you happy. During the course of time that you're together, ask her what is on her bucket list, places where she'd like to travel, and if she has sexual fantasies she would like to explore. It might be helpful to create a running list. Start jotting down places she'd want to visit, experiences you'd both enjoy, and timelines for doing these things.

Keeping an open mind extends beyond traveling and trying new foods; this also includes sexual fantasies. You can make your sugar baby ecstatic by being more adventurous in the bedroom. Learn new techniques or positions which you both would like to try. And be equally open to new techniques or positions that she suggests in the bedroom. Make her feel as if her curiosity and creativity is valued, as opposed to sticking with old school methods that show you're stuck in a rut. Fresh approaches and honest eagerness for innovation will certainly keep her coming back for more.

Remember, in most cases your sugar baby has "far less mileage" on her than your wife or ex-wife. Many younger girls these days are fascinated by the whole *50 Shades of Grey* fantasies. So, consider taking her to an adult store where you can purchase toys for the bedroom. Is she interested in a threesome? Have you asked her if she is bi or even bi-curious? If so, use this as an opportunity to introduce your other sugar babies to her and you can all have some fun!

IT IS ABOUT GIVING AND RECEIVING

When stripped down to the core, sugar dating is an arranged relationship. It's where you promise to do your part and she promises to do hers. Think of it as a "give and take" or "give and receive" arrangement. To keep your sugar baby happy, be prepared to maintain an open line of communication always. This prevents any misunderstandings that come from silence.

If you fulfill your part of the deal, she will also fulfill hers. Veteran sugar daddies report that a happy sugar baby is often willing to go above and beyond in all departments. In order to maximize your return on investment with your sugar baby, make sure you fulfill her needs. Trust me, she will reciprocate in many different ways. You're not a mind reader; so remember to ask when things aren't obvious. She may sometimes be shy to ask for something. (A shy sugar baby? Yeah, they exist!)

A happy sugar baby is the gift that keeps on giving. She will help explore your deepest sexual fantasies, cook for you the next morning, provide classy company whenever you travel, and even - fingers crossed - introduce you to her hot friends for some wild threesomes. It's up to you and your sugar baby to find ways to make sure that both daddy and his sugar baby are pleased.

KEEP OTHER SUGAR RELATIONSHIPS PRIVATE

Even though sugar relationships are essentially non-conventional, people may become emotionally invested. And that can risk going overboard. It's important to be vigilant when such dynamics occur - and to address them immediately.

Let's take the example of a sugar daddy that's seeing multiple sugar babies. If this is you, you should try your best to keep the other relationships away from your current one. (That is, unless your sugar baby likes girls and you've already discussed exploring multiple partners.)

This discretion should be consistent. It means not answering phone calls from other sugar babies in front of her. It means not bragging about your other partners. It means giving her your undivided attention every time you meet and not drooling over other girls passing by. Remember that your sugar baby is an attractive female who is accustomed to receiving a lot of attention. And not feeling that she's competing with other ladies for your attention.

The scenario will also depend on what your sugar baby is expecting. If she's open and okay with other partners in the relationship, then you can all have fun together. However, never disclose to one sugar babies what you're paying the other one. Avoid this subject at all times as it can lead to jealousy and unnecessary drama. It turns sugar babies into clawing cats.

While you are offering her something more than guys her age, she's still sensitive to feeling unappreciated. In fact, a sugar baby who feels this ongoing insecurity will rarely be happy when she's around you. If she finds out that you have other sugar babies you're giving gifts and attention to, dissatisfaction quickly creeps in. The irony is that she may also be seeing more than one sugar daddy, but she will still feel "jealous" of the unequal treatment.

The best policy to avoid jealousy in these situations is simply "don't ask, don't tell." If she's uncomfortable with your seeing other sugar babies, simply don't bring them up. Likewise, you should ask her not to talk about her other sugar daddies either. Keep the deep details of your sugar lifestyle private and to yourself. When you're with her, be with her, and put everything else on hold.

How can you do this? The most effective way is through proper scheduling of your own time. If you have reserved Wednesday nights for meeting with sugar baby A and Friday nights for sugar baby B, keep it that way and avoid switching things around unnecessarily. Also, be sure to set clear boundaries regarding your time and privacy. She should know when you're busy and should never text you back to back. Don't accept unnecessary jealous behavior. If it comes up, talk about it and reassure her about your commitment. If it happens yet again, then drop her like a bad habit.

DON'T PUT TOO MUCH EMPHASIS ON THE MONEY

There's a big difference between a prostitute and a sugar baby. Most guys struggle with this distinction. They think that the answer lies in the money and only the money. But it's a lot more than that. And if you can't shake that attitude, she definitely will pick up on your frame of mind. Making it all about the money might make her feel like a hoe. Nobody wants to feel like a piece of meat - even filet mignon. So your disgruntled sugar baby might simply decide to end the relationship abruptly.

So let's break down the difference. Hookers, prostitutes, and whatever else you want to call them, are primarily focused on the money. Hookers' motivating factor is money, so how much you pay is all part of the game. It's what you're willing to pay to play. Experienced hookers will have a full upsell menu they are willing to tease you with. Their services will be generous - so long as you keep the money coming. "Wham, bam, thank you ma'am" is the extent of this type of arrangement. When you're done, you're done - and don't let the door hit her ass on the way out! These girls also don't have much of a choice when it comes to who their customers are, provided they have the cash.

But our classier sugar baby likes genuine status, and she will reject any guy who doesn't make the grade. You see, sugar babies are of a different breed. Although money is an important factor, it's by no means the only motivation. Their concerns and cravings are a mixture of money, lifestyle, and discretion. Many sugar daddies will realize, to their delight and relief, that their sugar babies expected more than just money. The ladies expect a mature gentleman who will take care of them, spoil them, and give them a good time—possibly even mentor them, providing them with advice and guidance for their later lives once they have moved on.

Therefore, don't think that a fat wallet is the only thing that will make your sugar baby happy. If that's all you're willing to offer, then you might have messed up your priorities. Perhaps you're merely looking for a quick fuck from a professional sex worker vs. an authentic sugar baby. If you want a real, meaningful sugar relationship, then you need to do a little more work, such as seeing her as a real person and not a cash register. It will take genuine time and caring as you explore what she likes to do, join her in adventurous escapades, and honestly honor your responsible role as her bona fide sugar daddy.

MAKE SURE SHE'S COMFORTABLE

Perhaps the biggest obstacle that ladies face is not feeling a real connection with you during the sugar dating experience. The truth is that it can be hard for both of you. It means that you and your sugar baby need to drop the fortified walls we tend to put up out of fear, doubt, anger, or mistrust. For some, the fearful feeling of being hurt again can create a barrier or awkward tension between you and your sugar baby. Do your best to detect these emotions - in both you and her. And address them! Offer comfort and reassurance to your sugar baby.

However, if you notice that she's still a bit off or just uneasy, even after a couple of dates, don't hesitate to straight up ask her what is making her feel uncomfortable and find out what exactly is bothering her. Play therapist just a little bit. But if it looks like her neuroses go deep, you didn't sign up for shrink. You need to move on - and hope she gets the help she needs.

Remember to comfort her by giving her compliments and letting her know that you appreciate her. You should certainly avoid any derogatory comments which make her feel like a cheap whore. Respect her boundaries and don't rush into sex until you're both feeling chemistry with one another. Unwelcome high-pressure sexual advances are a sure way of making her feel uncomfortable. Don't be a savage and try and force the penile issue.

Sexual compatibility matters in your sugar relationship, and if it ain't there, you can't make miracles happen. That lack of sexual chemistry will eventually cause the death of the arrangement. You're a sugar daddy, not a sex therapist; you can only do so much! Save your sanity and move on.

WORK WITH THE INFORMATION
SHE'S WILLING TO SHARE

Most people fail to recognize the unique nature of sugar dating. It's nothing like your typical relationship experience where you endlessly share all of your deepest, darkest secrets with one another. In sugar dating, discretion is a major factor.

For example, you may have a family, you're recently divorced, or you're working in a field where your sugar dating behavior can damage your professional reputation.

Therefore, you may not want to share private information with your sugar baby at will. Imagine putting your secrets into the hands of the wrong girls; you can easily fuck over your livelihood and your life. You have to consider the possible pitfalls. In the event that you decide to cut off a sugar baby or limit her allowance, your sweet sugar baby might really be an evil bitch. She might have her revenge by blowing the whistle on you - to your wife, to your boss. To avoid being blackmailed, be sparing about the personal info you share. She's your sugar baby, not your confidante.

In fact, the same rules apply to your sugar baby. If she shares intimate details about her personal life, financial or career situation, you may feel closer. But you have also been burdened with powerful information into what makes her tick. Burdened because now you are also in a dangerous position to use that information against her if the relationship goes south.

As a result, it's best for you to both avoid being too nosy about each other's private life. Of course, it is natural to want to ask her questions and share information. This is a natural way to build trust and form social bonds. However, err on the side of discretion. Resist poking into her personal life and deflect any deep questions about family and career that she may ask. If there's something you feel you need to know about your lady friend, don't be afraid to ask. All she can say is, "I prefer not to talk about that."

The best approach to take is to just let her tell you what she cares to tell you. Don't pry. Don't cross boundaries to demand more. If she freely shares more, then that's fine. But if she starts giving away too much, ask her to put the brakes on her confessional. It's much better for the longevity of your relationship if she decides to only give you a sneak peek. Take it in stride and work with what you get. This hands-off policy will make it easier for the two of you to get along.

BONUS TIP

Some of these tips are pretty obvious. How about some out of the box ideas?

Here's **Jerry Bigs's 10 Ideas to Surprise and Delight Your Sugar Baby**

http://mysugarguide.com/outside-the-box

FRIEND ZONE IS AN INSULT

The "friend zone" refers to that awkward point in your arrangement where there is a mismatch in sexual energy between you and your sugar baby. It's a major roadblock to the sugar daddy mission. I seriously doubt that you have invested this much time into a sugar relationship just to have a "friend" - because you're not likely to blow fat stacks of cash on a friend. And you don't fuck a friend.

Sugar daddies who insist this is okay are not perceptive. They refuse to see that the mission has been aborted. Wanting to be in the friend zone with your sugar baby is backwards logic. It's the opposite of what the sugar relationship should be. To be blunt, it's lame, it's pathetic. And it's time to call it a day.

If you father in response to this bump in the road and linger in the friend zone too long, the harder it will become to break past this barrier and either jump-start or resume the intimacy with your sugar baby.

It sounds ironic that the previous section was about making her comfortable, and now we are talking about not being too passive. But hear me out: you need to put on your big boy pants, take the lead, and get out of the friend zone as quick as possible. Why? Well, if you find yourself in the friend zone, it's because of one or more of these factors:

- You're not attractive to her.
- You might be too dissimilar or not have a natural connection.
- You're too passive and are waiting for the right time.
- You're too fucking nice!

At the end of the day, it is better to put your best foot forward and be direct about what you want and expect. If she is not willing or interested, then it is better to simply walk away and find a new sugar baby who gets you heated up - and vice versa. After all, you have more than enough friends.

CHAPTER 12
CHALLENGE

I cannot emphasize how important it is to compliment your sugar baby. Seriously, compliments go such a long way. A quick story: I was at the bar the other night after a work event. I saw a perfect 10 knockout. I couldn't take my eyes off of her. So when she walked past me to the bathroom, I said, "Sorry to bother you, but you are absolutely gorgeous." She smiled, said thank you, and went on her way.

About 20 minutes later, she walked up to me on her way out, and slipped me a napkin with her number on it. Now if I had said nothing to her, I would not have this knockout's phone number! That's what it's about, my dudes.

Write out five smooth (not sleazy) compliments any woman would love:

1. ....

2. ....

3. ....

4. ....

5. ....

13.

SPICING THINGS UP IN THE BEDROOM

ow we get to the fun part. Let's talk about sex! It is fair to assume the majority of men entering the sugar dating scene are in it for the physical aspect. As you scroll thousands of potential sugar babies, perhaps you are envisioning some steamy scenes inside your head: wild one-on-ones, threesomes, or even some kinky BDSM.

Such steps need some advance preparation. It is best that you set the tone for the bedroom adventures with your potential sugar baby. Make sure you both have a mutual understanding before you get too deep into your arrangement. Don't be afraid to talk about sex and explore both your and her wildest fantasies. But proceed with caution. Keep in mind that if your sugar relationship is built entirely upon sex, the relationship may not last too long. Unless you can also kickstart some emotional connection. Some can. Most can't. That's life. It all depends on what means more to you.

UNDERSTAND THE SEXUAL DYNAMIC IN SUGAR DATING

Most men foolishly believe that sex in sugar dating is all about them. It's a false sense of entitlement; you give her the princess treatment and spoil her, so she must satisfy all of your sexual desires. But sex shouldn't be a one-way street. While it is important that you get to blow your load, your secondary goal should be to ensure that you please your sugar baby as well.

Even though men and women are both sexual creatures, the ways they get aroused are extremely different. Men who are instantly aroused, and a stiff dick knows no conscience - nor any discretion. Women are far more complex than us, so it's crucial that the sugar daddy takes his time to understand what works best for your sugar baby. Find out what it takes to getting her sexually charged.

Once you have that info, and you know the right buttons to push, your goal is to get out of selfish mode and give her pleasure. This will keep her coming back for more. Making an effort to understand what makes her tick - as well as moan and scream - will be worth the effort. You'll be able to look forward to these benefits between the sheets:

You will enjoy sex more

Let's not kid ourselves, fellas. You're studying up on your sugar baby's sexual temperature for a good reason. If she enjoys sex more, so too will you. If you actually care about her pleasure, you are that rare man, and she will appreciate your concern. Studies show that well over 50% of women have admitted faking an orgasm during intercourse or oral sex. Part of this fear of intimacy, insecurities about sexual performance, or the desire to hurry up. But a lot is because men simply don't care enough to take care of women's sexual needs. You are going to be the exception to that rule - and you will reap the benefits!

When you take extra care of your lady, you will feel a gratifying level of masculinity. You will also feel flattered as she reaches orgasm after orgasm. This added boost to your self-esteem will also improve your track record on the dating scene; you will never again feel insecure about approaching a sugar baby, because you will be wholly confident in your ability to please her in the bedroom. Good sex is, by definition, a win-win scenario.

Ways to keep her coming back begging for more

What better ego-booster is there than your sugar baby craving for more sex? You must be doing something right. You will be that rare man who takes the time to satisfy their partners. And that does not mean endless amounts of penetration, riding her thoughtlessly like a bronco. The bedroom wisdom offered by your friend Jerry Bigs will allow you to stand out from the rest of the guys who simply don't give two fucks about classy fucking. Here's a side benefit: In those occasional times when you don't have enough scratch to show her a good time on the town, a lusty roll in the hay will more than make up for it.

It will boost your overall confidence

Self-confidence is an important factor in sugar dating, but not all of us are overflowing with massive levels of self-esteem. How can you change this and boost your sometimes-fragile ego? One way is to simply forget about yourself altogether—and put her first. Think about it this way; if you keep your sugar baby sexually satisfied, it will boost your own level of sexual confidence. You get back when you give. You will feel good about yourself and your partner, making your overall venture into sugar dating a life-affirming experience.

WHY SOME MEN FAIL AT THE TASK:

Not understanding what women want

Some men fail to recognize that women are far more complex when it comes to sexual arousal. This might come as a shock, but a wild sex marathon, is not the key to most women's sexual satisfaction. Men simply fail to understand how to read nonverbal cues in women and how to properly interpret the difference between a friendly gesture and a sexual come-on. Here are some non-verbal cues you should familiarize yourself with. When it comes to communication, body language is king.

Touch and body language

A woman who's in the mood will have a more sensual style of touch that's different from her everyday behavior. One of the signs that she is interested in you is through "reciprocal touching" - that is, she touches you after you touch her. She may start to gently stroke your arm, your chin, or your shoulders. This touching and gentle caressing should send a signal to you that she's giving you the green light to go further. Touch is one of the most important things you can learn to master, hands down. You should never treat your sugar babies' personal space as public property, since everyone has a unique set of boundaries. The key to touch is understanding how to navigate the space between welcomed and invited contact.

Eye Fucking

Have you ever been "eye fucked"? No, this is not some crazy kinky fetish shit. This is when your girl makes direct and intentional eye contact, holds it, smiles, and then never stops. If a hot sugar baby is eye fucking you, the signal is crystal clear: she wants you to do something. You're getting the full-on come-on. Go for it!

Eye contact is always a good move, whether in flirting or in the sack. If you break eye contact when you're inside her, you can also send the wrong message to your sugar baby. During passionate sex, the last thing she needs is a faraway glance; it signals that you simply have no interest at all. This is the absolute most critical time for eye contact with your sugar baby.

Is she all smiles and laughter?

Smiles and laughing are some really simple ways you can gauge her level of interest and approval. Does she smile when she is talking to you? Does she laugh or giggle when you joke with her? Does she laugh at your dumb jokes? If so, then these are all really good signs that she is interested in you. A playful sugar baby might even give you a naughty, suggestive smile as a way of telling you she is down to fuck. The smile will be enhanced by long-held eye contact and playful touching.

Getting things started the right way

The brutal truth is that most men can go from cold to full-on erection in a matter of seconds. However, your sugar baby will prefer some foreplay. Foreplay is absolutely necessary for good sex. Your sugar baby deserves a little warm-up session to prepare herself for the main course of intercourse, both mentally and physically. As a sugar daddy, you need to come up with new ideas on how to maintain a vibrant sex life in the sugar relationship. And don't look to your sugar baby for a critique in the sack, so you know you are falling short. Frankly, most sugar babies will hesitate to bring up their dissatisfaction for fear of disappointing you and losing their "benefits," Therefore, most men are deluded into thinking they're doing everything the right way - while they perform miserably. Be pro-active and find ways to talk with your sugar baby about ways you can improve your sex life. But start out right and don't skip the foreplay.

Blowing your load too fast

Do you constantly shoot before you mean to? Sucks for you. Premature ejaculation is the fucking worst. You have to put a stop to this craziness right now, before you start getting a bad reputation by sugar babies who gossip too much. It's not about fucking continuously for hours; rather it's about being in control of your orgasm and knowing how to finish at the right time. Easier said than done, right? Luckily, there are ways to extend your sex time and come off as a sexual superman in the sack.

For starters, try daily Kegel exercises daily. Another thing to use stamina condoms, which contain a special lube to delay climax. Bonus: If you work things with your sugar baby effectively, you could bring her to orgasm much faster and not have to hold out for the hour-long sex marathon.

Anxiety and ED

Young or old, athletic or dad bod, we have all reached a time when our anxiety may have gotten the best of us, resulting in inferior sexual performance anxiety. There are many reasons for this: fear of poor performance, being self-conscience about your body, worrying about your dick not measuring up, and stress. Stress will cause your blood vessels to shrink, making it a chore for blood to flow to your cock. Your penis is now doing an imitation and your dick is going to be worthless as a wet noodle. No bueno!

How to cope? Get out of your head and get into the moment. Turn on some music and lower the lights. Focus on enjoying this pretty little thing right before your eyes.

If all else fails, go talk to your doctor and he can set you up with some meds. You have to nip this thing in the bud before it kills your sugar daddy career.

> Sometimes it's best to just listen to what your lady is telling you she wants. Why not do that right now...
>
> Here's **10 Sex Tips From a Sugar Baby**
>
> http://mysugarguide.com/sexy-tips

BONUS TIP

UNDERSTANDING THE FEMALE MINDSET

Believe it or not, women actually enjoy sex just as much (if not more) than men do. This is especially true for your hot little side piece who has chosen to engage in an arrangement with you. She understands that sex will be an expected part of this engagement. However, you need to dazzle her with sweet talk and saucy body language that will remind her that sex with you is a mind-blowing sexual experience. To make progress in this area, Jerry Bigs offers a guaranteed game plan to ensure that the sparks will fly. We call these the 4 C's of great sex:

Consent

"Yes means yes" and "No means no." It's a good idea for you as a sugar daddy to pay attention to words at the dinner table or in the sack. Make sure you know the difference between consensual sex with your sugar baby and a hard pass. Just because she was giving you a green light 20 minutes before, this red light is real. Heed it! Be sure that you never assume everything is okay. It is recommended even in the heat of the moment that you pause for a second and ask your partner if what you're doing is OK. And if your sugar baby isn't giving you a very clear "oh, yes," then you should be fully prepared to halt the grinding right then and there! That's called mutual respect and that's the only way I want my sugar daddies to play the sex game. Hear me, fellas?

Be aware that alcohol consumption can make matters muddy. But that doesn't excuse you from playing by the rules. It means making sure there is full consent before you both get wasted. Again, check in several times to see if her good mood is still strong, or whether it has vanished and she wants to reconsider this bedroom adventure. If you are ever in doubt about what's happening during sex, err on the side of the caution. It may be best for your relationship to shut it down and leave the adventure for another time. Better safe than sorry.

Comfort

If she isn't comfortable with you, then this isn't the time to lean in harder. It doesn't mean that the vibe will suddenly change when you lure her into bed. Your sugar baby in not your neighborhood whore. She definitely wants to feel comfortable with you before you go ramming your cock down her throat and smacking her ass. So how can you ease the tension and get relaxed and in the mood for some naughty fun?

It means backing up a little and perhaps revisiting the first days of courtship. Maybe you need another dinner. Or some sharing of stories. She needs to feel more at ease and believe that she is an equal partner in this arrangement. You need to reassure her twice as hard this time. Or this is never going to work. It is your goal to make her feel at ease, relieve the tension, and make her happy and appreciated.

Compliments

As a sugar daddy, you are more than capable of spoiling your sugar baby with gifts and an allowance. But an equally effective way - and one that doesn't break the bank - is to spoil her with genuine and sincere compliments. Show her with words that you appreciate her. The key to making this work is being able to strike a balance. You don't want to overdo it.

Be genuine and natural. Make her feel comfortable. Tell her you are really into her. Start off by complimenting her about her appearance. Even zero in on the areas that she considers her imperfections The goal is to show her that you appreciate more than just her lady parts. Casually learn to weave the compliments into your conversation without overexaggerating.

Also, avoid a negative or judgmental tone at all costs. Keep the subject matter bouncy; squelch any conversations regarding religion, politics, or race. Pay attention when she talks, rather than hijacking her conversation.

My final word on compliments is most likely she has heard them all before. But a sugar baby doesn't mind repetition in this case. So dish out the sweet words without holding back.

Care

Show your sugar baby that you actually care about her emotional well-being. This effort on your part will go a long way to forging a genuine connection. The idea is to show her that you are interested in her as more than just her tits and ass - even if those tits and ass are sheer perfection.

HOW YOU CAN SPICE UP YOUR SEX LIFE WITH YOUR SUGAR BABY

Ok, now that we got all of the necessary, boring shit out of the way, let's talk about sex. You might be thinking that you know it all and you have much more experience than your sugar baby. Well, that might be true. But those extra years you have on her also means you haven't learned any new bedroom tricks in a long time. So, maybe you will discover that she can best you in the bedroom. Swallow your pride and ask her kindly to share her expertise, as you are open to some innovations.

Here are several important steps that will ignite that fire between the sheets and keep your baby coming back for more. Try them all; you never know what will work because every sugar baby is different.

Ask her what she likes

Getting to know your sugar baby and her erotic tastes can be an adventure all in itself, not a grueling task. The idea here is for you to casually weave your "penetrating" questions into a natural conversation. You never want to blindside her with a random question like, "Do you enjoy anal sex?" This will make her think you only have a one-track mind.

While getting to know your sugar baby can be a fun time, you have to proceed cautiously with the sexual survey. Start by opening your secret book of passions.

What is your favorite sexual fantasy? Do you have any fetishes? Ask her how she feels about them? If she doesn't run screaming from the room, then ask if she is open to explore them with you.

Then zero in on her personal preferences. What turns her on the most? Does she reach orgasm from penetration or does she require additional stimulation? Does she enjoy giving blowjobs? Is she open to exploring threesomes? Does she like anal sex? Does she like sex in adventurous places? What kind of porn does she watch? Do you like sex toys? Is she into BDSM? You should have a good understanding of her sexual preferences.

It's also important to find out what she *doesn't* like. Positions that are uncomfortable or painful for her? If you're going to get at all kinky or experimental, it's important to be open with one another about hard and soft limits. Hard limits are things she absolutely refuses to do.

Soft limits, meanwhile, are things she's nervous about, never tried, but not necessarily opposed to. Maybe you're into choking during sex. She's not thrilled with the idea of being choked, but under the right circumstances, once you've established a bond of trust together, she might be willing to give it a try. Communication will lead to better, more fulfilling sex for both of you.

Cut the guesswork and tell her what you expect

The good thing about sugar dating is that you play by your own rules. There is no right or wrong so long as you focus on open communication. If you have taken the time to get to know the sugar baby's likes and dislikes and even fantasies, you should feel much more comfortable telling her what you want.

Honesty plus diplomacy are a great combination. Tell her exactly what you expect and don't be a pussy. Some sugar daddies want hot, wild sex while others prefer quality time over dinner or a relaxing massage. Just be sure to be yourself from the beginning. Personally, I love being able to tell my sugar babies what clothes I like and how turned on I would be if they wear them.

Under the right circumstances you can even suggest a naughty scenario where she does a number of role-playing scenes that are part of your preferred sexual fantasy. See how far she is willing to go for you! And then ask if you can return the favor. After all, sex between a sugar daddy and a sugar baby should be a well-traveled two-way street!

Let the Fun Begin

Getting your sugar baby all hot and frisky starts the second you initiate contact with her. For women, sex is more of a way of life than just a deed. **Think of her sexual energy as a point system and not a switch.** Your sugar baby will observe your every action as she adds up your "sugar score" based on several categories: the way you walk, smile, your style and the way you dress, your manners, your smell, your body language and, of course, your personality.

You want to do all the right things to score big - and to set yourself apart from the wannabes.

The wannabes are the men who can't get enough points to get past second base. Nor are they imaginative enough to see the wild side of their sugar baby. And that's a shame, because a prime baby will open up and rock your world. She may possess an appetite for sex that you would only see in porn movies. Get ready for sexual exploration on an unprecedented level.

For some guys, maybe your game might be a little unpolished. You simply need to learn to relax and summon all the charm and swag you need.

Need more reinforcements? Jerry Bigs is gonna take pity on you amateurs. I will share some insider tips on how you can ensure things get off to a good start.

A few basic guidelines: talk with a warm and welcoming tone, adapt to her level of energy, be sure to make eye contact, and smile at the right times.

No sugar baby wants to feel like a booty call, so it is your job to create an emotional connection before you broach the subject of casual sex. Really nervous and the words aren't flowing? I suggest grabbing a few cocktails first, as alcohol will surely act as a social lubricant.

CHAPTER 13
CHALLENGE

It's important to remember sex with a sugar baby is still a two-way street. Just because you're giving them gifts doesn't mean they are your sex slave. Here is where the 4 C's of Great Sex are most important, and will save the day.

Write out the 4 C's of Great Sex and what they mean to you.

1. C ....

What it means to me: ....

....

2. C...

What it means to me: ....

....

3. C...

What it means to me: ....

....

4. C...

What it means to me: ....

....

14.

DEVELOPING A MUTUALLY BENEFICIAL ARRANGEMENT WITH YOUR SUGAR BABY

The most important step towards an ideal sugar relationship is drafting a mutually beneficial agreement between you and your sugar baby. Remember, it's all about finding the perfect balance where you both are happy.

When you are ready to set up an arrangement with your sugar baby, be sure to stand firm in what you want and expect from her. As a sugar daddy, you are most likely cash-rich and time-poor. This means your sugar baby should be flexible with your busy schedule. This may put her on notice up front that you will not tolerate any flaky behavior from her, like chronic last-minute flaking out of a scheduled date. While both of your times are valuable, your time as a captain of industry is far more valuable - and your schedule far less flexible.

This is the time where you lay down some firm rules that will help you both respect each other and not abuse one another. This is not the time for a nonchalant attitude regarding the key parts of this arrangement: time of meetings, frequency, money, gifts, sexual desires, privacy, etc. Being crystal-clear now regarding your agreement will help steer clear of any potential misunderstandings in the future. (Not all of them, of course.)

It all comes down to *communication*. You should be willing to listen to her needs, show willingness to negotiate, and even be reasonable when she isn't. You're creating a contract of sorts for this arranged relationship that will hopefully skip the rough parts and petty jealousies of traditional relationships. The success is based on being fully clear about what she needs in terms of capital and what you need in terms of companionship. Simple enough, right?

This is your perfect opportunity to tell her what you expect from her: privacy, discretion, communication methods, allowance, frequency of meetings, the length of time you expect to spend, where you meet and more.

After this is all on the table, you can begin negotiating an agreement that is mutually beneficial. Ideally, you should hammer out all of these stipulations before you hammer her. Meaning, come to an agreement prior to any sexual encounters.

It's always suggested to discuss these details in person.

IT STARTS FROM THE FIRST CONVERSATION

Negotiating an agreement (sounds so official, right?) typically starts on your very first date. It's important to have this talk face-to-face during your date. Even if you may have bounced ideas off each other online, now is when you will really get to agree on some solid information regarding the relationship moving forward.

Believe it or not, there are sugar babies you will meet who will not seem like the right fit for you. How? They may not physically be what you had expected or their attitude or humor doesn't quite vibe with yours. It would make sense to confirm these incompatibilities up front before even starting to negotiate an agreement. That's why Jerry Bigs urges you to have a face-to-face meeting to establish whether there is promise on the air. After some small talk and a cocktail, you can now segue the conversation into specifics of the actual arrangement.

If this potential sugar baby still seems a bit hesitant, you have two options: You can negotiate further during subsequent dates. Or you can heed your gut and call it a day now before you expend any time unwisely. Remember that ratio of sugar babies to sugar daddies is in your favor!

BONUS TIP

From meeting once a week to being your "girlfriend" at a wedding. Here's the arrangements that work for most men.

Here's **Five Common Sugar Dating Arrangements That You Can Cop**

http://mysugarguide.com/ideal-arrangements

WHAT SHOULD A TYPICAL AGREEMENT INCLUDE?

When you have already filtered out the non-ideal girls, it will be so much easier to develop arrangements. Whoever remains is more willing to negotiate and take the deal you offer. There's no need to complicate things. At the end of the day, if you can offer what the sugar baby needs, voila, you closed the deal.

Now it's time to draft a detailed arrangement. Strong verbiage helps to avoid future misunderstanding and disagreement. Because, frankly, who wants to go back to the drawing board with another sugar baby if you don't have to? Let's take some time to study these important agreement points that prevent unseen troubles.

Allowance

Negotiating a monthly allowance with your sugar baby is actually fun if you like playful negotiating. Remember, let her state her number first. If she wants less than what you intended to give, then congrats, that was an easy deal. If she thinks she's the shit and demands more than what you are willing to give, then you need to up your game. Sell her on how your potential sugar relationship will benefit her more than you and let her know that she can have other things more valuable than money such as your mentorship, your connections, your time.

I know *most of you* will lose your damn mind when you talk to a chick with a banging body that is way out of your league. I know because I'm also guilty. Dude, hold on to your dick and let your brain think for a second. You don't want to be thrown off your game as you negotiate.

Be mindful for potential problems in her demands. If you're married, her living her best life could cause bank account problems. It could be so obvious that even your wife sees the suspicious spending and unusual withdrawals from your bank account.

If she lives out of state and tells you that she needs money to buy the plane ticket to see you, you could be swindle dicked out of hundreds if she decides to go missing. If she wants a $5,000 allowance and your budget is $2,500, are you smart enough to get up from the table and walk away? Or will you try too hard to reach a compromise, not realizing that she will try to push that total back up in a month or two? Then you could find yourself tapping into your savings.

But you are one smart sugar daddy who isn't going to be hoodwinked! Why? Because you were wise enough to purchase this book. You're now ten times smarter than the average sugar daddy!

Now you are aware of this type of devious sugar baby behavior so you can call her out on her bullshit when she tries to use you. Don't be a sucker! Elite men are not suckers. Use your brain to think, not your dick. There are plenty of hot, broke chicks out there. If she's playing hardball from the start, ten to one that she'll be kicking you in the balls down the road soon. Once again, tuck your dick out of sight and focus your mind. Know when to negotiate and know when to walk away, brother!

We have already discussed the "pay-per-meet" option. It's more convenient because you won't have to waste your time negotiating an ideal allowance with someone who might not last a month. Plus, "pay-per-meet" means you won't have to worry about her going "missing in action" with your money.

Payment preferences

You should have a solid plan in place for how you will send money to your sugar baby. This method should be discreet, especially if you're married and share finances with your partner. Bank transfers can easily get you caught if you're trying to keep your sugar affair private. Cash is always a great option for you and your sugar baby (if you trust her). There are a lot of money transferring applications that are discreet and reliable. Sugar daddies prefer these common apps for moving sugar baby funds:

- *PayPal:* All you need is her PayPal email address
- *Cash App:* All you need is an email address, phone number, or username
- *Venmo:* All you need is an email address, phone number, or username

These next couple of tips are for married guys who would like everything to be safe and discreet. To be extra private, you can create another account from your main account on CashApp or Venmo and add a separate reloadable card (i.e: Vanilla gift card) into the account and transfer money from there. If you want to leave no trace, send crypto currencies. Coinbase, Binance, BitPay are some common apps that you can use.

Where to meet when sex is involved

The first few meetings with your sugar baby should be in public places. You may have initial meetings at a café, over dinner, or even at your local pub/bar. When an arrangement starts and sex is part of the deal, you need to agree on a private place to meet.

The most common is her place, a hotel, or your place. Are you comfortable enough to meet at her place? Is she comfortable enough to come to your place? A lot of sugar babies don't like hosting because they have roommates, boyfriends, or live with their parents. A hotel is an option, but if you're local then it's not the most ideal place to be seen, especially if you're married.

If you decide on a hotel, be careful how you pay for it. You can give her cash to pay for the room, or she can use her own credit card and you can refund her. (This might be a better option after you've established trust.) Another idea is to have a separate, personal credit card for such uses, or a prepaid card that you put money on, as needed. This will make it less likely that you get caught. And make sure to pick a hotel far from a shopping mall or where you live. It's never good to have too many eyeballs looking at you on a secret date.

If you're single and have a private home, your goal should be to eventually work this in. Hotels can become expensive over time. Besides, if you have to go to work the next day, it's such a hassle to pack a suitcase with all the essentials and clothes to change into. Make sure you have a safe or lockable cabinet where you can hide your valuables when inviting her over. Trust no one.

Meeting at your place is easy for you as she can come over and leave after the date. But you have to also be concerned about sharing your address. If the sugar baby gets too attached, she might surprise you by showing up without notice. This can get quite awkward if you have other sugar babies over.

Time and Frequency

You should mutually agree on a set amount of time for every meeting, especially if your schedule is hectic. Setting a meeting frequency will help you determine the allowance amount. It also makes scheduling dates easier for a busy executive like yourself. And if you're married, you definitely need a set schedule. Work this out with the sugar baby from the beginning and it will save headaches in the future.

Communication Methods

This part is for married guys only. Watch out for minor things that can cause big problems. Don't be sloppy and get caught by the wife by using the same iCloud account on all your Apple devices. They will sync all your iMessage. Worst case scenario? Your sugar baby decides to get drunk and blow your iMessage up - and the wife sees it. There are messaging apps that you can use to send secure and encrypted messages such as Telegram, WhatsApp, Confide, Signal, Wickr, etc.

And more importantly, make sure to use a secondary number (Google Voice or iPlum) when signing up on these apps and exclusively communicate with the sugar babies in the apps from the very beginning. That way they can never blow your iMessage up while you're out and the wife is home suddenly hearing dozens of "dings" from the iPad.

CHAPTER 14
CHALLENGE

Communication is key, right? Tell it all, brother. The best way to get what you want is to tell your sugar baby. She's a looker, not a mind reader. You gotta communicate what you want. Great. Now, do you know what you want?

Answer the following questions as quickly as you can. Try not to think too hard:

What do you want: ....

....

How much do you want to spend: ....

....

How often do you want to meet: ....

....

Where do you want to meet: ....

....

These may not be the best answers, but they are a start. And usually your gut instinct is the right one.

15.

WHAT IF THINGS GET SERIOUS?

O h shit! Did you plan for the relationship to escalate? Maybe yes but mostly no. We all sugar date for a singular reason: #nostringsattached. But here's a warning up front: A sugar relationship can get serious without a moment's notice. How in hell does that happen?

Well, it begins innocently enough: A date or two, enjoying each other's company, good conversations, and exciting sex. If you've followed all the Jerry Bigs tips given in this book so far - and why the hell wouldn't you? -- you will most likely end up with a sugar baby who is happy, comfortable, and eager to keep things going. You've done your job right!

Now, what if you have done too good of a job!??

As you continue to grow closer, don't forget to double-check your emotions and arrangement status. Ask yourself these questions:

"Are we still on the same page?"

"Are we more intimate than we should?"

"Has the vibe gone from casual to clingy?"

"Is she making a move towards a relationship?"

Reviewing these reality checkpoints will help you realize when things get serious between the two of you. Most importantly, you don't want to end up in a situation where you are practically dating without a mutual agreement to change the dynamic. You may not have taken the time to discuss boundaries, future goals, and how you will communicate with others. Well, buddy, now's the time! Because a lopsided situation will result in disagreements moving forward.

So what should you do if you realize that things are quickly getting serious? Glad you asked. Jerry Bigs has your back.

CONSIDER YOUR FUTURE GOALS AND BE HONEST ABOUT THEM

First step: Make sure you both are on the same page before looking any further into the future relationship. A relationship happens when two individuals come together not only to love each other, but also to work towards mutual goals. That's why defining and communicating your goals is a must. Now let's dig into the details.

Defining your goals

The strength of this relationship will largely depend on your future goals. Are they the same? That's the key to harmony. There's a lot to consider here, so talk it all out sooner than later. Topics for debate from your end: Whether you wish to be married, whether you're already married and are willing to divorce to make room for this sugar-baby-turned-bride, whether you want to live together.

She also has a lot to think about on her end. How will engaging in a relationship with you affect her future goals? Where is she financially? Does she want to be married in the near-future? Switching from a sugar relationship to a serious, long-term relationship is a pretty drastic change. As we've talked about already in these pages, she's a sugar baby because she has goals she wants to achieve. Will marriage and family disrupt these goals? If so, is she okay with that?

Start with an honest assessment of your future goals, sugar daddy. As the senior member of the arrangement, you probably have a more settled life. Topics for discussion: Does she want kids? Do you, if you already have some? Are you willing to walk down the aisle again? Or do you prefer an open relationship? In this case, gentleman go first and state their wishes. Because, frankly, you have a hell of a lot more at stake! That's not sexist; just accurate.

She may have entered this relationship simply to help pay for college, and now she finds herself in love with a man much older than her. What should she do? Younger women (and younger people in general) don't always have a firm game plan. They are often not sure of what lies ahead. Or they are more likely to change their minds quickly, running away from a commitment. She may not be picturing herself ten years later, while you have a vision for life to retirement and beyond, being an astute businessman.

If you're already married, and/or seeing multiple sugar babies, a long-term relationship will cause multiple problems. Does she expect you to be monogamous? Are you willing to be? If you came to her because you were bored with your wife, how would she know you won't get bored with her one day, and move on to the next sugar baby? If your wandering libido has been a problem in the past, it will almost undoubtedly be a problem in the future.

Communicate your goals

Maturely discussing the above questions with brutal honesty will help you move closer to solving this tough issue. Write down the answers if need so you can really know how you feel. It's often more instructive to see the truth in black and white.

When things get serious, both of you should openly talk about your future goals and plans. Give yourselves plenty of time to be open and honest before taking the next step. It is now the time to exchange answers and discuss options without judgment.

In the case that you know you're going to continue to want sex or other companionship outside of your relationship, you might consider an open relationship. Here you can both get the extras you need, while remaining committed to each other. If she's not comfortable with that, then maybe this relationship isn't a good idea after all. On the other hand, if you're absolutely positive that she's the one, and your wandering eye will wander no more—you're going to have to give her major assurance. This may mean one hell of a prenup.

COMING CLEAN TO FRIENDS AND FAMILY

The next issue you may face if you decide to get serious is what you will tell friends and family. They may be understanding souls, but this is extraordinary stuff - so they may have a million questions. The first will be how you first met. Ouch.

Telling them that she was your sugar baby may put some in a coma. For others, it will immediately turn on their judging mode. If you want to keep things easy with a white lie, then rehearse your alibi in advance. It's totally fine to lie to people who don't need to know your business – but the stories have to match.

Some people will think she's a high-class hooker who's with you for the money. Even if you both know it's not the entire story, how much time and energy should you summon and explain to everyone? So coming up with a well-orchestrated story in advance to ward off unnecessary harassment is critical. Here are some clever fabrications – don't call them alternate facts, fer Chrissakes – that you should practice telling about how you first met:

- **Club/bar**: Always a convenient explanation. Clubs and bars attract all sorts of people, so it will reduce curiosity levels.
- **Work conference**: Saying you met at a conference denotes a responsible and formal meeting place, which is socially accepted. It also suggests that she has her own life and career.
- **Via a mutual friend**: This works well if you can get a mutual friend to play along. But make sure you pick a friend not widely known within your circle.
- **Online dating site**: Everyone is using online dating platforms nowadays to find their partner, so it won't surprise too many people.
- **Airplane or airport lounge**: You've probably have heard stories of couples who met at the airport. You're one of those success stories now.

Most people will stop asking when you give them a believable story. If they keep being over-curious, then make up an obnoxious and incredible story just to mess with their heads. But trust me, most people will be satisfied and move on with their lives – unless they are your spouse or children. They may need additional convincing. If you don't trust yourself enough to maintain the charade, then just shut down all questions.

> **BONUS TIP**
>
> The best advice comes from those who lived the experience.
>
> *Here's* **5 Stories of Things Getting Serious and How They Worked Out**
>
> **http://mysugarguide.com/real-serious-stories**

If you and your smokin' hot sugar baby agree to be polyamorous, then you have to consider if you want your friends and families to know about your unique relationship. They may get very confused if they see you out on a date with someone else. If you have the balls to show off all your women, then good for you. God bless! You probably can stop reading this book now.

But for those of you who are CEOs, executives, public figures, or very publicly married in a high-profile power couple arrangement, and want to keep your public image conservative, then keep reading. Jerry Bigs's class is still in session.

CHAPTER 15
CHALLENGE

It doesn't happen often, but you may become deeply involved with a sugar baby. If that's the case and you plan to introduce her to family and friends, you might want a back story...

In 3 to 5 sentences, write a believable story of how you met your sugar baby. Make it something you would feel comfortable saying to people.:

174 | THE SUGAR FACTORY

....

....

....

....

....

Good! Again, it may not happen often, but people like to pry – and it's always good to be prepared.

MAINTAINING YOUR PUBLIC IMAGE TO THE OUTSIDE WORLD

uring the course of your sugar relationship, you can't avoid being seen in public together. People you know will spot you at a restaurant or the movies. If you think that no one will eventually ask questions, wake up! People are extremely nosy. The larger the age gap between you two, the more the questions they will pepper you with.

There are two methods you can use to tackle the situation. Method one: Tell them to fuck off and enjoy your date. Method two: Go ahead and give a damn. Tell them your made-up story about your girl and how you have met. It's not necessary to give them a full, honest detailed story about your arrangement or relationship because people will still think what they want to think.

Just keep in mind that people will continue giving you unwanted attention, so how are you going to handle it? You certainly don't want your sugar baby to feel uncomfortable; neither do you want to be pestered with annoying stares and judgmental looks. You could avoid crowds by staying inside, but you would soon get cabin fever locked away in your hotel room or home with your sugar baby. Here are some Jerry Bigs-approved suggestions to keep it cool while in the public eye:

Develop a story

Developing a believable story is the easiest way to keep people off your back. Sit down with your sugar baby early on and develop a narrative that works for both of you. "Who is she?" She could be your friend, assistant, nurse, personal shopper, etc. "How did you meet?" The safest answer is through a mutual friend because they will stop asking at that point. If they ask for a name, use some friend who most people have heard of, but do not know. Or find a true-blue friend who will lie for you and corroborate your fairy tale.

Whatever your alibi, please don't pretend she's your family member. That shit is just *weird* and will cause many problems down the line. Just remember, if you're going to have a cover story to explain your "perfectly innocent relationship," you'll need to keep everything rated "PG" in public. It helps make things easier to explain.

Choose your meeting places wisely

To avoid running into judging acquaintances, you could seek out tucked-away places that are less popular. If the trendy restaurant downtown is packed with your co-workers and neighbors on any given night, choose a location off the beaten path. Seek out places that are dimly lit and have private booth seating as opposed to an open table layout. Restaurants inside hotels and resorts are also a good option because they are usually five-star quality and filled with tourists, not locals. You could also take trips out of town and explore new meeting places.

> 💡 **BONUS TIP**
>
> Stay creative with your dating and your sugar baby will stick to you like glue.
>
> *Here's* **Jerry Bigs's Out of the Box Ideas for Date Night**
>
> **http://mysugarguide.com/date-ideas**

If your sugar baby has been in the game before, she may know of many awesome places for a private meetup. The important thing is to adapt your activities to hang out in environments where fewer questions will be asked:

- Don't meet at the bar you go to three nights a week.
- Don't get couple massages at the regular spot.
- Don't take her to company events and wonder why people are nosy.
- Avoid posting photos together on social media.
- Book different seats than your annual ticket seats at a local game.

Little details like that will save you a lot of unnecessary stress and worries along the way, especially if you're also in a traditional, committed relationship.

HATERS GONNA HATE

If you both have nothing to lose, then who cares? Society is always too judgmental anyway and you don't have to answer to anyone.

Haters hate, so let them hate. You just have to know how to ignore them. Or toughen up and get used to people talking behind your back. If she can also develop a thick skin, even better; then carry out your regular plans without a care in the world. Embrace who you are, have the time of your lives, and it will be mission accomplished. In the end, most of them are probably just jealous that they aren't shagging a hot young woman. #Truth

---
CHAPTER 16
CHALLENGE

You can't hide those prying eyes. But you can outwit them. Rather than take a date to your favorite spots, do some legwork and find some out-of-the-way places for your romantic rendezvous.

List five lesser-known places you can take your sugar baby on a date without gawkers who know you:

1. ....

2. ....

3. ....

4. ....

5. ....

17.

TIPS FOR SURVIVING THE SUGAR DADDY LIFESTYLE

Why survival? Because while the sugar bowl scene is sexy, emotionally rewarding, and exciting, it's not for everybody. Not all men in sugar dating can keep up with the routine. It requires honesty, ingenuity, and open communication. So they have fallen out of the game. This mostly occurs when such men dive into the scene without a plan and learn things the hard way.

BONUS TIP

When things go bad, it can get awkward. Just take these men's stories for example.

Here's **5 Sugar-Dating Horror Stories and How to Avoid Them**

http://mysugarguide.com/horror-stories

Sugar dating is like driving a speedboat through the open ocean. Can you keep control and avoid toppling over? Can you maintain the speed? Can you afford the maintenance if the engine gets too hot? There are a lot of things you need to consider as you enter the sugar bowl and negotiate an arranged relationship.

Luckily, you have a cheat sheet that you can use (this fucking book in your hands, numbnuts). And you have the top sugar daddy authority - me, Jerry Bigs. This is an unbeatable combination to ensure that you connect with the choicest sugar babies - and that these attractive young girls don't drain your bank account while you're swooning. Ecstasy should go hand-in-hand with intelligence. Surviving the sugar dating scene involves having the following in check:

Make sure you can afford it

Remember that your sugar baby will expect to be spoiled every so often, and she may also need a monthly allowance from you. These expectations can be met if you have the resources. If you don't, the lifestyle can easily cause you a lot of stress. After all, no man wants to be considered as having failed. Therefore, the most important survival tip is to make sure that you can afford life in the sugar bowl once you've gained access. Find someone who fits your lifestyle, budget, and interests. If she asks for a $10k allowance and you can't afford it or don't want to give her that much, be firm. Smile broadly and say "no sale." Or, if you have a steel will, then invite her to negotiate. But then she might think you are simply frugal - another word for cheap.

Don't be too nosy

It is said that women are clingy and often get too attached, while men are aloof and care-free. It's true, but not entirely true. Men can be very needy and jealous, especially if the woman is intelligent, attractive, confident, fun, and balls-to-the-wall sexy. (Did I mention sexy?)

In sugar dating, you can easily become wrapped up in emotions regarding your sugar baby if you're not careful. Understandably so because she is hot and not yours. Be on your game at all times, because other sugar daddies could sweep her off her feet when you start losing your grip.

To survive the sugar dating scene, you need to keep a clear head, restrained emotions, and suppress clingy tendencies. Promise yourself to stay out of her personal life as much as possible. Give her space; most sugar babies maintain a separate personal life that may include a boyfriend closer to her own age. (And that guy most likely doesn't know that she's also a sugar baby.) Or she may live at home with parents, or roommates (none of whom know about her sugar lifestyle).

There's no reason to know what she's doing when she's away from you - and being nosy can be a recipe for disaster. Think of it this way: how would you feel if she started asking you personal questions about your wife? Or your coworkers and friends? It would probably make you feel uncomfortable. The best guarantee for a vibrant sugar relationship is to avoid being involved with her other life. If she wants you to know something, she'll tell you.

If you start having deeper feelings for her and feel the itch for more than just a sugar arrangement, slow down. First, you need to see if she is on the same page. If she is, then you'll need to change the rules of engagement in your overall relationship dynamic. (See Chapter 15).

If she doesn't want to take this deeper, you have two choices:

One, you suck it up and stick to the existing sugar baby agreement. Yeah, right; that's like asking someone with a sweet tooth not to eat the chocolate bar within reach on the counter. You've developed deeper feelings and you can't pretend they are not there. Even if you are a good pretender, your yearning for her will come out in ways that will become obvious. Jerry Bigs recommends that you take choice two: That's breaking it off and letting her live her life, and not get guilted into your obsession.

You are free to get back on the sugar run and find another sugar baby. But hold on a minute, brother. Listen to Jerry Bigs. What makes you think you will be able to honor those specific keep-it-casual boundaries next time? What makes you think that you may not fall for the next sugar baby and will lobby her to get deeper?

Reality check: Maybe you're just not cut out for the casual sugar arrangement. And that's okay. Take yourself out of the running and go after something where the ground rules allow for romance and will make you much happier. If you don't, then you may be looking at stalker charges - and you don't want to deal with a judge's restraining orders.

Don't get too attached

When I say don't get too attached, I mean "Are you ready to let her go if you have to?" In sugar dating, **objectivity trumps emotions**. You both have your own personal lives and goals. The sugar relationship is primarily meant to address certain limited needs you both have. You want a fun, relaxing time and great sex, while she wants the same, plus financial support for her personal needs. It can be easy to become attached to this young and attractive girl because it's all fun and stress-free, but it's best not to.

Her goals may be very different from yours. For example, a sugar baby who needs help with college tuition will most likely move on with her own ambitions once she graduates. It's understandable for her to have her own plans. That's why it's called *an arrangement.* Make sure you always have a plan B ready in case she decides to take a different path. Yeah, you love, love, love her - but it's not going to work. Save your energy, save your sanity, and dive back into the sugar bowl.

You need a certain resilient mindset in order to win the sugar dating game. Accept that it's temporary, and that you are not in charge. Of course, it's also possible that sugar babies might get attached to you. You're an established, successful man who is also a source of steady income for her. You may also be a mentor to her. And if you're handsome, she may see it as a score.

Here's where you need to offer tough love and tell her that something deeper will not work out. Again, she may insist that's okay and that you can resume the casual arrangement. But be real about this; she has already spilled the beans, and she can't just put her feelings back into the genie bottle. You'll be doing both of you a favor by ending the relationship and wishing her luck.

Bottom line, fellas: To survive in this rewarding but exceedingly regimented scene, there are two primary rules: You don't get too attached to her, and she doesn't get too attached to you. End of story.

Maintain a certain level of control

In sugar dating, you will have more control than in a conventional relationship. After all, you have the money and you're the older one in the arrangement. And since it's an arrangement, everything is negotiable. If you know how to negotiate effectively, you win. Be prepared to step up and be the alpha dog - the one who controls where things are going. If your sugar baby is young, innocent, and open-minded, you may be expected to take the upper hand always. That means you're the one to decide where most dates take place, how often you meet, and how the relationship will grow as you explore new things to try. You are also the one to open a discussion if either of you are unable to agree on what was initially decided upon.

In order to survive, have fun, keep an open mind, but be vigilant when you don't seem to be on the same page. Of course, you will seek her input in major decisions but make sure to let her know that you're the decision maker. The level of control you need will depend on your sugar baby's personality and age. Sometimes, aggressive sugar babies can end up controlling your actions in an unfavorable manner, in which case you should beat a hasty retreat and block her. On the other end of the spectrum, very laid-back sugar babies are like dating corpses. Find someone who lands in the middle for the best give-and-take dynamic.

WHEN IS IT TIME TO CALL IT QUITS?

ike all good things in life, a sugar relationship might eventually come to an end. There may be a number of different reasons for this, some caused by you, others caused by her, and some that are the fault of no one in particular.

RED FLAGS AND WARNING SIGNS

If you are paying attention, there are red flags that signal things are not going as smoothly as they used to be. You can save yourself a lot of time, frustration, and heartache if you learn to spot these flags early. And act upon them. To use nautical terms, if you ignore red flags, then you may just crash into an iceberg that will sink your love boat.

Sometimes, but not always, if you recognize a red flag early, then you can fix it and save the relationship. But other times, there is just no way to fix things; your relationship is on a collision course with reality that is inevitable. So get ready to abandon ship!

Here are some of the most common red flags to watch out for:

You no longer enjoy her company

You love black raspberry ice cream. But who wants to eat fifteen bowls of it in one sitting? Ditto for perfect relationships. You start out wanting to be with her all the time. And maybe you even come close to that. But then you wear out your taste buds for this sugar baby. You get bored with the same flavor, day in and day out. You start craving other flavors.

Over time, you may begin to lose interest in your sugar baby. She may have been exciting at first when you were caught up in the excitement of the pursuit. But now that you have what you wanted, the stakes are no longer so high. You find yourself getting lazy in keeping the relationship interesting. She once seemed full of engaging conversations, but now seems distant and disengaged. Most puzzling is that her rockin' sexy body no longer spikes your automatic boner like it used to. It's the downside of being together a lot. You simply grow accustomed to her, and that leads to boredom.

However, if you are still interested, but she seems bored and is killing your vibe, you could find out what's happening. It is always a good idea to first understand why she's acting the way she is. It could be a personal challenge that she's facing, a temporary hurdle at work, or the worst-case scenario is that another man is vying for her attention and has her torn between two sugar daddies.

If she wants to talk about it, you can see if you'll be in a position to help. If not, keep your distance but show your support. Remember not to become overly invested, as this is not a traditional relationship. You're simply showing an effort to keep things going, especially if the juice is worth the squeeze.

If her change in attitude completely turns you off and every meetup becomes too emotionally cold or too transactional, don't hesitate to call it a day. Set her free and set yourself free, too. That's the perk of not being married to the sugar baby! You don't have to suffer when things become sour. But be a gentleman to the end; meet with her and calmly explain that things are not going as expected. Or if she has proven unhinged, then call it quits with a gentle but firm text.

Here are red flags that indicate there is a problem that may spell the end for your time together in the sugar bowl.

The sex falls flat

It sounds a bit harsh to simply say that you're in it for the sex, but sex is certainly an important component of sugar dating. If the sex falls flat, this is a red flag indicating that things have gone from red-hot to code blue. Bedroom matters are always sensitive to discuss, even in sugar dating. It could be that she is no longer doing her part and she avoids having sex with you altogether. It could also be that she makes it feel like a chore and is not helping in spicing things up. It could also be your "fault" where you're not paying attention to her needs and are not satisfying her in bed.

If the lackluster sex is on her end, this may be due to many different reasons. You can try to talk to her about it and to mention that the sex has recently not been meeting your expectations. This book has an entire section that addresses bedroom matters and gives you practicable tips that can help you ignite a fire between the sheets.

However, if sex is dead, then you can't raise a corpse. Face it that it's time for a new playmate. Start the auditions now!

She only cares for her needs

Occasionally you will notice that she focuses only on what you can give her. It may feel like she's only in it for the money and gifts. If so, she may be too spoiled and selfish to hide the truth. That's when it becomes obvious; she may bug you constantly for her allowance or complain about gifts. The power balance has been upset - probably irrevocably. Because how do you teach her humility or gratitude? And why the hell should you? That's not what you signed up for.

Remember that sugar dating is an agreed-upon pact where both parties uphold certain roles and responsibilities. If she changes her tune and only cares about her needs, be ready to rehearse that final conversation before you exit her life. Don't waste time trying to reason with her; she has shown you exactly who she is.

You go broke

This is an obvious red flag. If her constant demands for designer things has emptied your wallet and she's now starting on your bank account, it is time to call it quits. Sure, sugar dating is expensive by nature. And you can only stay in the game so long as you have the big bucks to play. But a considerate sugar baby will understand the boundaries of your income and play within the guidelines for the most part.

Many sugar daddies that experience a change in disposable income think that they can simply wing it until things improve. However, this will not work if she's a brazen, gold-digging sugar baby. She won't accept the fact that the game has changed momentarily, and that she needs to briefly lower her expectations. It is better to be honest upfront and tell her that things are now different on your end. Then expect her to head for the door.

You get too attached

In most cases, getting too attached is a recipe for disaster. You're in a sugar relationship for a reason. Getting too emotionally involved can complicate things and speed the collapse of your arrangement to end. When you're blinded by emotions and she's not on the same page, things get out of control. And since she has the power to stop things, this can be difficult to accept for a successful alpha male. What's worse is that you're older and being rejected may bruise your ego.

We've talked already about what to do if you both find yourselves wanting a more serious relationship. But what if you do, and she doesn't? You might think you can simply continue the arrangement as normal despite your feelings? *Stop!* It's a bad idea. The longer you continue, the more your feelings are likely to grow. Better to break things off now, rather than risk things getting out of hand down the road. This is the benefit to a non-traditional arrangement; you can jump ship if it's not working and not have any paperwork, divorce, or family disapproval!

While she's said no to a more serious relationship for the moment, you may think you can still shower her with gifts and ultimately change her mind. This is a very big mistake. Why? Your ego will not tolerate it, nor will your wallet. Remember: She's already said no! Avoid the temptation of becoming too attached and get out early! There's always another one waiting for you.

Sugar Babies have red lines, too.

Here's **Confessions of a Sugar Baby: Red Lines Not to Be Crossed**

BONUS TIP

http://mysugarguide.com/red-lines

KNOWING WHEN TO STOP IS AS IMPORTANT AS KNOWING HOW TO GET STARTED

The sugar dating life can be addictive. Enjoying sex with no strings attached, exploring new places with hot companions, and experiencing new bedroom adventures can become a drug that you never want to let go of.

But too much of a good thing is not always good thing. As you enjoy this sugar bowl lifestyle, you should also have an exit strategy. Know that it probably won't last forever. Nothing really does. And it is equally possible that your sugar babies will eventually move on with their goals and plans. You want to make sure that you're not stuck in the same place for too long. Keep a clear perspective of your personal and professional goals. This way you can always make sure that sugar dating is not holding you back.

While this is undoubtedly a fun and exciting lifestyle, the choice is yours in knowing when it's time to pull out. As long as you're always consciously in control of your decisions, you should be in good shape. If you forgot to establish boundaries, then you should be seeing a shrink.

CHAPTER 18
CHALLENGE

Do you have a few non-negotiable deal-breakers? Behaviors or actions that you just can't tolerate from your sugar baby, no matter how smoking hot she is?

List five deal-breakers that will definitely end the arrangement with your sugar baby:

1. ....

2. ....

3. ....

4. ....

5. ....

It's good to know your limits, and better to know when they've been crossed. People are unpredictable and can change at a moment's notice. Stay sharp, my friend.

19.

WATCHING OUT
FOR SCAMMERS

The world of sugar dating is full of unique surprises. No surprise; the financial aspects of sugar dating attracted unscrupulous people with bad intentions. Stories of fakes are becoming increasingly common across various sugar dating sites. These scammers pose as either sugar daddies or sugar babies and they use slick tactics to solicit money from innocent members. Not good.

Let's look at some of these scams and learn to protect yourself from falling into these traps.

SUGAR BABY SCAMS

As a sugar daddy looking for a hot companion, you are an easy target for scammers who pose as attractive sugar babies to trap you and separate you from your dough.

While most sugar babies on online sugar dating platforms are genuine, some are looking for ways of making a quick buck. Let Jerry Bigs teach you how to recognize a sugar bowl scammer.

Asking for money before the actual meetup.

One of the most common sugar baby scams involves the girl asking for money even before your first meeting. Once you begin interacting with her online, she may give off an impression that she really likes you and is ready to engage. Very quickly, she may ask for money to fix her car, her phone, or catch up on rent.

This should raise a red flag right away. It's a scam! They usually target older guys whose physical appearance is below average and seem to be in desperate need of attention. The fake babies will flatter the hell out of you in a quest to empty your bank account.

Do not send money if you run into this situation! The scammer may even sweeten the deal and say that "she" needs the money to pay for gas to drive to you. Don't fall for it! Instead, offer to reimburse her for the money once she shows up. See how quickly she evaporates. The excitement of potentially meeting with this hot chick can cause you to make deeply wrong-headed decisions. Any genuine sugar baby will be willing to meet with you before asking for a money transfer.

Remember what we talked about in Chapter 10: Unless otherwise explicitly stated, the first meetup typically involves no money, and no sex. This is for your protection as well as hers. You need to make sure she's not trying to scam you. If she asks for money before meeting up, say no. If she insists, block her. If it seems too good to be true, it probably is.

Requests for account/banking information

Another common mistake people make is to provide sensitive information to their potential sugar babies. Many scammers are experts at making you feel comfortable enough to share your banking information, credit cards, social security number, etc. As you know, this leaked information can cause lasting damage, such as identity theft, instant bankruptcy, and divorce.

It's always a good idea not to share sensitive information until you can be sure that you can trust your sugar baby. Nowadays, there are many different channels through which you can transfer money without sharing your personal information, such as PayPal, Cash App, Venmo, etc.

Asking for webcam meetings

A new scamming technique being used by scammers is to arrange for a webcam session. This often sounds exciting because you get to see your potential sugar baby and she may even promise you a private dance. However, be wary of webcam sessions with someone you don't trust. There are sugar daddies that have been recorded nude on webcam and their "sugar babies" threaten to share their naked pictures on the Internet if they don't pay up.

If you do end up getting blackmailed with compromising pictures or video, here are the steps to take:

- Do not pay them.
- Pretend you will pay and ask for information on where to send the money. Then share that information with authorities.
- Try to record them threatening you with your iPhone recording app.
- Tell them you're not afraid (even if you are) and you're going to contact the authorities because blackmailing is a crime.
- If they keep on pressuring, ask local law enforcement to handle the matter.

If you stand up to them right from the start, they may realize you're not an easy target and just disappear. They are cowards and will simply move on to the next victim.

Being scammed face-to-face

Just because you've met your sugar baby face to face doesn't mean that you still can't be scammed. There are cases where sugar daddies meet with their potential partner and the girl insists on being given money from the beginning of the conversation. Then she abruptly ends the meeting, pockets the money, and insists she has an emergency she needs to rush to. That's total bullshit and you have just been burnt.

There are also guys who've had their wallets emptied during a night at a hotel with their newly met sugar baby. It happens when they went to the bathroom. It's always a good idea to remain vigilant at all times when you meet your sugar baby for the first time.

SUGAR DADDY SCAMS

Why should you care about sugar daddy scams? Good question! Because these scams will reflect badly on you, too. A sugar baby may be on the defensive and on the lookout for scams while searching for the ultimate daddy. Savvy sugar babies will demand you prove that you are real. The burden is on you to prove to them that you're the real deal.

Don't believe it? Google "sugar daddy scams." Voila! These scammers know their craft and know exactly what to say to make girls believe them.

Naive sugar babies may trust men too much, too fast. By knowing the dangers that are out there, you, as their mentor, you can help them better protect themselves in the future. Here are some of the most common sugar daddy scams that you should be aware of:

Issuing of False Payments

One of the most common scams against sugar babies is the issuing of false payments. The scammer pretending to be a sugar daddy asks the girl to get a reloadable prepaid card from her bank such as the Chase Liquid card and he will mail her a check to deposit, usually with a big sum or allowance. The larger the amount, the easier it is to trap the newbies. Little does she know the check is fake. As soon as it is deposited, with the right information, the scammer can withdraw the funds from an ATM and run away with it. After a few days, the check will bounce and now the naïve baby owes the bank the full amount that the scammer withdrew.

If a sugar baby ever mentions this situation, advise her to run as far away as possible from the dude, report his account, and immediately block him. And you, the new hero, might gain some extra love for saving her ass.

Requesting sensitive account information

Another way scammers operate is by asking their sugar baby to share account information so they can transfer funds. Unsuspecting sugar babies may end up having their banking information, credit cards, and social security number compromised. With current, up-to-date and secure money transferring apps, there's no reason to ask for bank information. Again, if your potential sugar baby brings this situation up, tell her that she can either play dumb to mess with him, then block or give him false information to waste his time, then finally report his account and block him. Either way, he will get nothing and you, her real potential sugar daddy, will get extra credits!

Asking the girl to buy him a gift card(s)

Sounds ridiculous, right? What kind of "sugar daddy" would ask a broke college girl to buy gift cards for him? And how the hell could the girl say yes and fall into his trap? Unfortunately, there have been multiple victims across various sugar dating platforms falling for this fraud.

Remind your girls to never buy potential sugar daddies a gift card. We're rich. We can buy them ourselves!

THE FINAL WORD

I know I just dropped a big bomb in the sugar bowl with that scammer shit. But don't get me wrong; the sugar dating scene, when done well, is a joy for everybody. It's a refreshing alternative to the manacles of marriage and the other traditional relationships we get ourselves caught in.

Bottom line: There is so much good stuff ahead for the sugar daddy who learns his lessons, polishes his behavior, and acts like a gentleman. But not a fool.

But remember this: **This is not a lifestyle everyone can handle.**

I've made it in the sugar daddy life because I am smart and wealthy. How wealthy? I'm a self-made millionaire. I can switch out the toilet paper in all my mansions with $100 bills and it wouldn't make a dent in my bottom line.

I easily spend $1,000 on meeting a new sugar baby for the first time - and I don't even know if I want to keep her yet! If she's one of my favorites, I'll drop anywhere from $2,000 to $5,000 on an afternoon or night out.

To be fair, I spend more because I like to spoil my babies. But this kind of money isn't far off from what most sugar daddies spend. That's why I'm going to share one of my biggest - and final - secrets with you. Because Jerry Bigs is a good guy, and don't you fuckin' forget it or I will kick your ass from here to next week!

The info in the link below is what took me from making good money as a sports writer to making money that gets elite sugar babies to drop their wet, diamond-encrusted panties.

This isn't just sales pitter-patter; the info in this link is invaluable. I'm trusting you not to show it to anyone else.

The information here will very literally change your financial life. But you need to take the time to understand it and apply it because when you jump into the sugar bowl, you need to be at the top of your game in every way.

That includes - but is sure as shit not limited to:

- How you manage your time - your most valuable resource.
- How patient you are with your sugar babies.
- How stacked your cash flow is.

Because no matter what a badass sugar daddy you turn out to be, the reality never changes that *these women have options.* You need impressive resources to keep them happy, and that requires both generosity and ingenuity - because a whole bunch of zeroes in your bank account is not the only thing that makes the sugar dating scene hum.

My guess is you don't have that mega-bucks sugar daddy-level income yet. But don't worry, fellas. At the end of this section, I'm going to give you something out of the goodness of my heart: a special gift I made only for the people who bought this book.

But if you're not fully convinced you need a god-tier cashflow to attract top-notch sugar babies, then I want you to think about lions. That's right, lions.

Look at lion prides. All the lionesses are *always* horny for the king of the group. Why not the other male lions, who work just as hard as Mufasa to bring home the gazelle meat?

Because Mufasa is the biggest and toughest and *strongest* motherfucker in the group. He is *the* alpha. Thus Mufasa drowns in lion pussy while lonely Scar jerks off in the hyena cave. Circle of life.

That's why sugar dating is almost strictly a multi-millionaire thing. It's not about ego; it's just how the game is played.

So if you're a doctor or lawyer or single business owner relying on a single revenue stream and want to play the sugar bowl, I got a bit of eye-opening news for you: It's time to step up your game.

All of those jobs are perfectly fine. But the reality is that even millionaires are limited by their income to see any success worth their time and money in sugar dating. So if you want to play, you're going to need to either lower your standards or level-up your life.

And I'm serious here. For your sake, **don't** become another broke hundred-thousandaire fronting as a multi-millionaire. Your dates with supermodel-quality babies with a taste for the finer things will drain your bank account in no time at all. End result? The masquerading sugar daddy will be left looking and feeling like a chump. And since sugar babies gossip, your name will be mud all over the sugar bowl and you'll never be taken seriously again.

But you get the picture. Sugar dating is next-level stuff that will, in all likelihood, require you to rise to the occasion - or fall out of sight. Face it - if you wanna compete in the Tour de France, then you better start doping. These big-boy games have big-boy rules, brother!

If you already feel stuck in your income bracket, and don't know how to break out, well - I'm about to become your favorite person in the world. You're gonna wanna kiss my ass from here to next week.

Now, I like you. I like you because you are smart. How do I know? Well, you're smart enough to know a good book when you see it. And that's why you have *Sugar Factory* still clenched between your eager mitts.

So I'm going to help you get over this financial hurdle and acquire some serious fiscal fitness - so you can quickly get down to spoiling your sizzling hot arm candy.

Here is your map to the pot of gold over the frikkin' rainbow. To be specific, here are eight investor's niches that will explode your income growth. That is, *if you know how to play them right.* (I did, and that's why I'm swimming in moolah.) They are:

- Forex
- Penny Stocks
- Sports Betting
- Crypto Training
- Crypto Trading Bots
- Credit & Points Hacks
- 7-Figure Amazon Training
- Crowd-Funded Real Estate
- Crowd-Funded Venture Capital

Listen up, greenhorn. If you want that ultra-elite, six-star lifestyle with the babes to match, you'll need to get out there and hustle. And I know you can do it. You already had the presence of mind to buy and read this book.

BONUS

Jerry Bigs's Secret to Big Money Success
http://mysugarguide.com/big-money

Now…getoutthereandknock'emdead.No,waitaminute.First, tellfivefriendsaboutthisamazingbookofmine.Afterthat,youcango out there and knock 'em dead. After all, you shouldn't be ungrateful!

Your faithful friend, the king of the sugar daddy world,

Jerry Bigs

THE CAPTAIN

P.S. When you land your first sugar baby, join us at the Sugar Sells mastermind group on Facebook and share your story!

P.P.S. Fuck it. I'm feeling extra-generous right now. So, do you have a question about sugar dating or how to go about making the money to play? My personal email is *jerry@jerrybigs.com.*

It may take me a few days to ping you back, but I will answer. Again, this is my **private** email. Do not share it with anyone. Unless you know some top-tier sugar babies looking for some fun times with a fun guy.

www.ingramcontent.com/pod-product-compliance
Lightning Source LLC
Chambersburg PA
CBHW071958090426
42740CB00011B/1987